The Political Economy
of Appalachia

The Political Economy of Appalachia

A Case Study in Regional Integration

Monroe Newman
The Pennsylvania State University

Lexington Books
D.C. Heath and Company
Lexington, Massachusetts
Toronto   London

Published simultaneously in Canada.

Printed in the United States of America.

International Standard Book Number: 0-669-84335-0

Library of Congress Catalog Card Number: 72-3556

To:

I. & J.K.
R.Z.N.
E. & H.Z.

Contents

List of Figures

List of Tables

Foreword

. Among the many federal programs chartered in the 1960s, perhaps the most innovative in concept and hopeful in application was initiated with the passage of the Appalachian Regional Development Act in 1965.

In the authorization of the Appalachian Regional Development Program, the Congress recognized that economic growth within the Appalachian Region would not be stimulated by standard federal programs for categorical purposes. The Region had serious deficiencies in its transportation system, education, health care, and other public facilities to which national programs were being applied. However, because of the peculiar and unique problems of the rural, resource-based economy of Appalachia, the development of such facilities required coordination and acceleration to not only meet specific categorial needs but, in the process, to induce, support, and sustain private investment and thereby economic growth.

The Regional Development Act recognized that a coordinated public investment program for Appalachia required the involvement of state and local public officials, as well as the public, in a new and different administrative structure. The Appalachian Regional Commission, state development offices, local development districts, and other public and private institutions were formed and have evolved to fill this role.

The keystone of the Program is the concept of a regional investment strategy set by the Congress and carried out by the Appalachian Regional Commission, participating state governments, and other responsible agencies. That strategy was to concentrate the expenditure of federal funds and the state and local resources required to match them "in areas with significant potential for future growth." The concept of realizing the potential for long-term economic growth of Appalachia, while in the process responding to many immediate human needs, was a monumental challenge.

In the following pages, Dr. Newman, who was a key participant in this process, provides a lucid and candid appraisal of the way this challenge was met.

This analysis is particularly timely, not only because of the continued need for surveillance of the Appalachian Development Program, but also because the program serves as a model in the continuing search for institutions and strategies to meet the critical national problems of an economy in transition. This book should be read not only by students of the subject, but by public officials and other policy-makers.

Senator Jennings Randolph

Preface

This book originated from a deep sense of gratitude and dual feelings of obligation. I am grateful to all those at Penn State and at the Appalachian Regional Commission whose cooperation has enabled me to be a continuous participant in the Appalachian development program since early 1964.

This opportunity also imposes obligations. As the only economist to have been continuously associated with the program, I owe an obligation to my colleagues to provide whatever professional insights I can that may enhance their ability to study and evaluate this and similar programs. Certainly, my evaluations cannot be taken to be those of a disinterested and dispassionate observer. But they are the judgments of a professional participant and have the merits, as well as the demerits, of participation. My explanations, analyses and evaluations are therefore offered as evidence for incorporation with those of others into the process of professional inquiry.

My other obligation is to the people of this country, and particularly those in the region. They have invested in Appalachia and deserve to know what was done and why. But beyond that, they deserve guidance for the perfecting of similar future endeavors. Some lessons learned in Appalachia may have wide applicability and utility. An obligation exists to distinguish those from others of a more parochial or less useful nature.

Contributions to this book came from the literally hundreds of people at the commission, in federal, state and local government and in private capacities with whom I have had contact. Their understandings, responses and perceptions were the source of continuous enlightenment and, sometimes, amazement.

While this book was in process, I was also assisting the commission in preparing an internal evaluation, the "Evaluation of the Appalachian Regional Development Program," soon to be released; some pages of this book were initially drafted as contributions to that effort. The staff members of the commission who worked on the evaluation, and the panel of outside readers created by the commission read, edited and improved my submissions to ARC. Their specific contributions to this book have been lost in mounds of drafts but are no less real for being unidentifiable. They have my sincere thanks.

More fundamental but even less identifiable contributions came from two others. My wife, Ruth, provided the patience, insights and infinite adaptability that has allowed me to live a double life as professor and regional developer. Edwin G. Nourse has provided intellectual nourishment throughout that has helped me to maintain the difficult stance of a professionally participating observer.

Drafts of the ARC evaluation were available to the Advisory Commission on Intergovernmental Relations. Its report, "Regionalism In The Federal System," therefore reflects the work done with the Commission staff on the internal evaluation.

The last word in the subtitle of this book may give pause to some people. "Integration" has become associated with our civil rights problems. In its use here, it is intended to emphasize the two-fold task of the Appalachian Commission: to meld a diversity of governmental units—local, state and federal—into a working regional entity; and to enhance the opportunities of the region's residents to participate fully in our evolving national economic and social life.

I willingly accept responsibility for the errors in these pages, but I am also eager for those errors that are there to be discovered and explored. I believe there are things to be learned from the Appalachian experience and if errors are found in my analyses, it will be because others have examined the experience too.

The Political Economy
of Appalachia

1 Introduction

Prior to Congressional enactment of the Appalachian Regional Development Act (ARDA) in 1965, this country had never attempted a multi-program approach to the problems of relatively low income areas that addressed these areas as an interrelated, contiguous group. Prior attempts had generally dealt with each depressed area separately. Underlying the Appalachian program was a belief that common causes were producing the afflictions that accompany relative poverty.

In addition to conceiving common causes, the program also visualized common interests between the relatively wealthier, adjacent areas within the region and the poorer areas whose plight stimulated the initial public interest. In fact, the higher income areas are the keyholes through which the strategy of the program seeks to unlock a future of wider opportunity for all the region's residents.

This book focuses on the program for the region—its immediate antecedents, the structure of ideas that influenced its composition and constitution, and the operations, alterations, effects and implications of the experiences of the intervening years. One premise that is basic to the entire presentation is that public policy is a blend of technical and political feasibility. Neither has been nor can be the sole determinant of policy. It is for this reason that the book returns so frequently to an examination of the range and validity of our conceptual understanding. Experience is our most significant laboratory for deepening and elaborating our technical and political concepts. The chapters that follow are, in a sense, designed to present a participant's lab notebook report.

A second basic premise is that the Appalachian experience may be a guide to the evolution of public policy and that the lessons that can be generalized from it should be open for inspection as critical public decisions are being made. As evidence for this belief, within a month of the last week of March, 1972, when these words were written, Senator Montoya of New Mexico introduced a bill intended to create development commissions that would regionalize the entire United States;[1] the Vice President, speaking for the President, encouraged the governors of the states to establish regional commissions to deal with a range of public issues;[2] and the Presidential Commission on Population and the American Future urged the development of "growth centers" (a key Appalachian concept) to diminish the nation's population distribution problems.[3] All of these events reflect favorable evaluations of the Appalachian experience and confidence that wider applicability is feasible and desirable.

1

The next chapter of this book provides an initial factual background for the discussion to follow. It presents an overview of some social and economic characteristics of the region, a brief summary of the ARDA's provisions, and a brief description of the internal operations of the agency charged with primary administrative responsibility, the Appalachian Regional Commission.

Chapter 3 briefly recounts past policies designed to assist areas of distress and describes the context in which the present effort was designed. Judgments about the effectiveness of past policies and the contemporaneous regional conditions were two important sources of influence on the program proposed. Another important source of influence was the state of theory and knowledge about the process of regional development, discussed in Chapter 4. The concepts then receiving widespread acceptance provided the intellectual basis for the program's design. As already mentioned, one important element in a full comprehension of policy development and implementation is the interaction between political possibility, statistical "reality" and conceptual understanding of the process to be influenced. Examining this conceptual framework is the primary focus of this chapter.

Chapter 5 is devoted to the interweaving of disparate influences into a strategy for regional development. Numerous strategy alternatives always hypothetically exist. In the case of Appalachia, they ranged from suggested depopulation to recommendations of repopulation. Within this range, a blending of many strategic alternatives yielded the one employed. Understanding the bases for the selection made is an essential element in an evaluation of the strategic decisions reached.

The strategy adopted places heavy responsibilities on state and Federal agencies for choosing among considered alternatives. This process is the essence of planning. The nature of planning in the Appalachian context, its objectives, methods and accomplishments, are discussed in Chapter 6. There the point is made that regional planning can take numerous forms, sometimes with very general and occasionally with very specific objectives. Decisions concerning the nature of the objectives had to be made case by case, followed by the considerable task of designing and conducting the planning process to achieve the objectives desired. Bases for judging the Appalachian planning experience are provided in Chapter 6.

The next one, Chapter 7, deals with the institutional mechanisms, the organizations, that labor in behalf of the region's residents. The principal aim of the chapter is to provide a basis for evaluating achievements in institutional development and performance. No legacy could be left to the region that would be more beneficial than concerned and responsive government at all levels.

A strategy based on planning by governmental agencies is expressed ultimately in expenditures. Consequently, Chapter 8 reviews where the money has gone, how it has been spent, and what factors influenced the thousands of separate decisions that lead to the pattern observed. In the short run, at least, a program is judged by what it does obviously, and the record of Appalachian expenditures provides an important basis for evaluating the labors of those involved.

The last chapter gives some inklings into what it all may mean, not only for Appalachia but for the nation at large. Neither the evidence nor our ability to interpret it allow unqualified assertions of success or failure but these years have yielded insights that may have utility beyond the present program and its geographic scope.

2

The Appalachian Experience: A Factual Background

Appalachia is the home of about 18 million Americans. Many of its residents may be surprised that they are citizens of what has been called the largest concentration of depressed levels of living in the United States. They may attain incomes and living standards in excess of the average for their fellows, so that they feel no personal relative deprivation. The physiography of much of Appalachia, with its valleys and ridges and hidden hollows, tends to make it easy to miss visual contact with less affluent fellow citizens. They probably do not share the psychology of deprivation, that blend of stunted mental and physical growth that thwarts ambition and is a common precondition for a willingness to accept public assistance. But they are Appalachians nonetheless. Congress has defined Appalachia as consisting of 397 counties[1] in 13 States, extending from southern New York State to Northern Mississippi and from the border of New Jersey to within a few miles of the Mississippi River (see figure 2-1).

Regional Overview

As table 2-1 indicates, more Appalachians live in Pennsylvania than in any other state, and on the average, the poorest Appalachians live in Kentucky. The national per capita income was $3,425, so that only in the 3 counties of Appalachian Maryland does average income exceed that of the nation, a situation that did not exist for Maryland or any other Appalachian state in 1960.

Outside Appalachia in 1960, 72% of us were urbanites and only 7.3% lived on farms. The remainder (20.8%) were rural non-farm residents. For the region, the comparative percentages were 47.5% urban, 9.7% rural farm residents and 42.8% rural non-farm residents.[2] The simple comparison of these sets of percentages says much about conditions in the region.

On the average, and contrary to much popular impression, Appalachia is a highly manufacturing region and not dominated by mining. For the region as a whole, a larger proportion of employment is in manufacturing than is true nationwide, and mining is not a dominant source of employment regionwide. However, there are states, such as Kentucky, which have a heavy component of mining employment and do not begin to approach the national proportion of employment in manufacturing. Of the regional labor force of 6.9 million in 1969, 3.9% were unemployed, a figure that probably understates the actual proportion. As is true nationwide, rural areas tend to under-report their

5

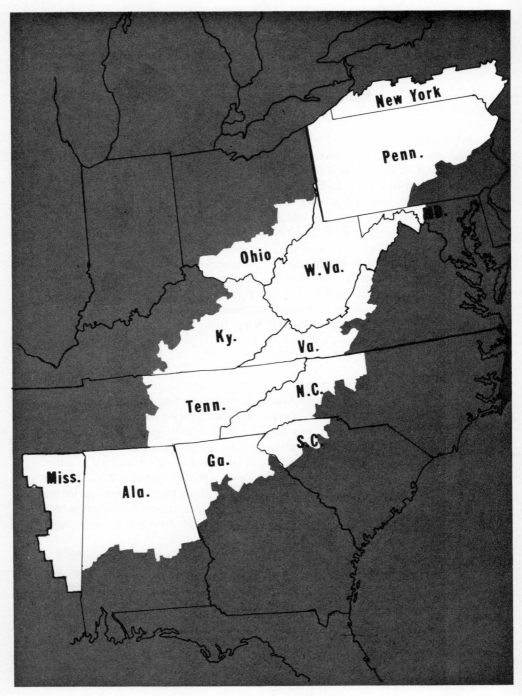

Figure 2-1. The Appalachian Region.

Table 2-1
States' Population and Income

Appalachian Portion of:	Population—1970 (thousands)	Per Capita Income—1968 (dollars)
Alabama	2,137.3	2,523
Georgia	813.6	2,063
Kentucky	876.5	1,717
Maryland	209.3	3,622
Mississippi	418.6	2,072
New York	1,056.6	3,200
North Carolina	1,037.2	2,594
Ohio	1,129.4	2,424
Pennsylvania	5,930.3	3,096
South Carolina	656.2	2,758
Tennessee	1,733.6	2,549
Virginia	470.1	2,057
West Virginia	1,744.2	2,583

Source: Appalachian Regional Commission, *Appalachia: An Economic Report—1970*, pp. 85 and 92.

unemployed, and in areas of deficient employment opportunities, those who do not seek work because of their belief that search would be futile tend to be under-counted. The comparable national reported unemployment rate was 3.5%.[3]

Programs and Administration Under the 1965 Act

When it passed the Appalachian Act in 1965, Congress found that the region, "while abundant in natural resources and rich in potential, lags behind the rest of the Nation in its economic growth and that its people have not shared properly in the Nation's prosperity. The region's uneven past development, with its historical reliance on a few basic industries and a marginal agriculture, has failed to provide the economic base that is a vital prerequisite for vigorous, self-sustaining growth." Congress stated the purpose of the legislation in these words—"to assist the region in meeting its special problems, to promote its economic development, and to establish a framework for joint Federal and State efforts toward providing the basic facilities essential to its growth and attacking its common problems and meeting its common needs on a coordinated and concerted regional basis."[4] Special note should be taken of two aspects of this statement of purpose, the emphasis on *economic* development and on the provision of *facilities*. Without any change in this legislative language, time has produced a shift in these emphases as later chapters will recount.

Under the act, the commission is given an extremely broad range of functions, a more narrowly prescribed set of programs to administer and general guidelines under which they are to be conducted. The act tells the commission, in Sec. 102, that it is to:

1. develop, on a continuing basis, comprehensive and coordinated plans and programs and establish priorities thereunder, giving due consideration to other Federal, State, and local planning in the region;
2. conduct and sponsor investigations, research, and studies including an inventory and analysis of the resources of the region, and, in cooperation with Federal, State, and local agencies, sponsor demonstration projects designed to foster regional productivity and growth;
3. review and study, in cooperation with the agency involved, Federal, State, and local public and private programs and, where appropriate, recommend modifications or additions which will increase their effectiveness in the region;
4. formulate and recommend, where appropriate, interstate compacts and other forms of interstate cooperation, and work with State and local agencies in developing appropriate model legislation;
5. encourage the formation of local development districts;
6. encourage private investment in industrial, commercial, and recreational projects;
7. serve as a focal point and coordinating unit for Appalachian programs;
8. provide a forum for consideration of problems of the region and proposed solutions and establish and utilize, as appropriate, citizens and special advisory councils and public conferences.

The specific programs authorized, their general nature and the cumulative funding available for each in the first six years of operation (through fiscal 1971) are indicated below:

Sec. 201 Authorizes the funding of a development highway system and of local access roads—$2,090,000,000.

Sec. 202 Authorizes the creation of multi-county demonstration health projects and limited funding of their operating deficits—$120,900,000.

Sec. 203 Authorizes the establishment of programs of land stabilization, conservation and erosion control—$19,115,000.

Sec. 204 Authorizes the fostering and support of timber development organizations—$600,000.

Sec. 205 Authorizes programs to remedy the scars of past mining practices—$33,385,000.

Sec. 206 Authorizes a regional water resource study to be conducted by the Corps of Engineers—$5,000,000.

Sec. 207 Establishes a revolving fund to assist the provision of low- and moderate-income housing—$4,000,000.

Sec. 211 Provides additional support for vocational education facilities—$91,000,000.

Sec. 212 Provides additional support for sewage treatment facilities—$7,400,000.

Sec. 214 Provides funds that enable the Commission to reduce the financial burden on communities that must match federal grants-in-aid—$214,830,000.

Sec. 302 Authorizes the Commission to support research and demonstration projects and the expenses of local development districts—$22,850,000.

An additional $5,876,000 was appropriated for administration.

In conducting its activities, the commission is told that it must be guided by some general considerations, in addition to specific ones incorporated into the individual program sections of the act. Generally, the commission is told by the law that its investments "shall be concentrated in areas where there is a significant potential for future growth, and where the expected return on public dollars invested will be the greatest" (Sec. 2). It is told that when it considers programs and projects, and gives them priority ranking, it must consider:

1. the relationship of the project or class of projects to overall regional development including its location in an area determined by the State to have a significant potential for growth;
2. the population and area to be served by the project or class of projects including the relative per capita income and the unemployment rates in the area;
3. the relative financial resources available to the State or political subdivisions or instrumentalities thereof which seek to undertake the project;
4. the importance of the project or class of projects in relation to other projects or classes of projects which may be in competition for the same funds;
5. the prospects that the project for which assistance is sought will improve, on a continuing rather than a temporary basis, the opportunities for employment, the average level of income, or the economic and social development of the area served by the project.

In addition, it is proscribed from providing financial assistance to relocate establishments, finance industrial facilities or activities, finance the generation of electric energy, and the transmission or distribution of electric energy or natural, manufactured or mixed gas.[5]

Administration of this law is the responsibility of a rather unique instrument, the Appalachian Regional Commission, a non-federal agency in which the federal government and the 13 Appalachian states participate as equals.[6] The legislation provides for a commission composed of the governors, or their representatives, of the 13 states and a federal co-chairman appointed by the president. The commission establishes basic policy by resolution. Action by the commission requires the federal vote plus the votes of the majority of the states. A veto exists on both the federal and state sides of the table, therefore, and there is also a "little veto" in the provision that no action or project can be undertaken in any state without its consent. It is noteworthy that no federal or state veto has ever been cast at a commission meeting and that most actions are unanimous.

The Federal Co-chairman

The Appalachian Act provides for presidential appointment of a federal co-chairman of the commission with a rank equivalent to that of an assistant secretary. His major roles, as specified in the act, are that he must approve any commission action and he is responsible for liaison with all federal agencies, particularly with the Office of Management and Budget and the Office of the President. In practice, liaison with other federal agencies has been largely handled at the staff level. When higher level policy coordination is required it is handled in *ad hoc* consultations with the cabinet officer involved.

The federal co-chairman has a personal staff of about ten people, all compensated entirely out of federal funds. The budget office for the commission is part of the federal staff and the preparation and presentation of the budget request for federal funds is done by the federal co-chairman with the advice of the states. He represents the administration's position on commission matters before Congress, particularly in the case of the budget. In presenting the federal share of the commission budget to Congress, he acts in a manner analogous to that of a regular federal agency head.

The commission has had four federal co-chairmen and the law also provides for the appointment of an alternate.

Member States

The states have the other half of the commission's policymaking authority. The laws say that the state members may be the governor or his designee or any person designated by state law. A strong tradition has developed that the governors are the state members. They participate in commission activities at the major policy level, but in every case they also select an officer to represent them at regular commission meetings. The law provides that the states elect a state co-chairman from among themselves. This has always been a governor. The governors serve six-month terms as state co-chairman of the commission.

State Representatives

The officer appointed by the governor to represent him on the commission is called the state representative. These representatives or their alternates attend the commission meetings and cast their states' votes on policy issues. In most cases these officers are also in charge of the administration of the program in their states. Usually they are cabinet level officers and they have a small staff at their disposal for Appalachian matters. The state representatives and their staffs are the focus for the program in each of the Appalachian states. They are responsible for the preparation of the state development plans, project applications, and work with regional federal agency offices, local governments, and the state agencies involved.

States' Regional Representative

One continuing concern in the administration of the Appalachian program is how to keep the commission program from becoming "federalized." The danger arises because the federal co-chairman is a full-time officer in Washington, the center of staff operations. A major staff activity involves contacts with federal grant-in-aid agencies so that the staff, and the entire commission operation could fall into a pattern of operating essentially as a federal agency. The states decided that they needed to retain a full-time representative at the commission to handle their affairs between commission meetings and to advise the states on policy matters coming before the commission. They established the office of states' regional representative, an action not required by law.

An ARC resolution describes the states' regional representatives as the "functional equivalent of the federal co-chairman" and he speaks for the states collectively when the commission is not in session. There have been only two states' regional representatives. The states' regional representative has a personal staff of four people. He and his staff are compensated entirely by the states.

Executive Director

The commission's staff operations are headed by an executive director, whose position is provided for in the act. He is responsible for developing policy and program recommendations to the commission and for general administration.

The Executive Committee

Early in the program, the commission created an executive committee to handle major personnel actions not delegated to the executive director. Over the years, the executive committee has become responsible for many more of the commission's major executive and policy actions between monthly meetings. The executive committee has been delegated most of the financial and administrative responsibilities that have not been delegated to the executive director. The members of the executive committee are the federal co-chairman, the states' regional representative, and the executive director, who has no vote. Therefore, actions of the executive committee must receive the affirmative votes of the federal co-chairman and the states' regional representative, voting on behalf of the states. Among the most important activities of the executive committee are the approval of projects and state plans. The executive committee does not usually meet to take these actions. The executive director proposes in a memorandum that the executive committee take a specified action on a project or state plan. It is then routed to the states' regional representative and after his approval to the federal co-chairman. Meetings occur to handle disagreements.

The executive committee also develops and discusses the agenda for commission meetings and develops program policy questions for presentation to the commission for resolution.

The Staff

The commission now has a staff of approximately 100 people. The relatively small size is made possible, in part, because many of the administrative and technical problems related to the commission operations have been delegated to federal agencies, and in part because of a decision by the commission to keep the staff small. The primary roles of the commission staff are program development and assisting the commission with project review and approval. The staff is now paid jointly by the federal government and the states and staff members are not federal employees.

The principal officers under the executive director are the deputy director, and the general counsel. The former is responsible for the administrative and public information units, and has also been delegated primary responsibility for the health, education, and early childhood programs of the commission. The general counsel is responsible for legal and contractual work and is the commission's legal counselor.

The remainder of the staff is divided into three operating divisions. The Division of Program Planning and Operations is responsible for program analysis and long-range plans for the development of the Appalachian region. That division is also responsible for evaluating the current commission program. The Division of Program Development contains professional experts covering the fields of commission programs and interest. It has experts in education, health, child development, community development, public administration, natural resources and other fields. The primary function of this division is to assist the states in developing programs called for under the Appalachian Act. Finally, the Division of Program Operations is responsible for the liaison with the states and for the review and recommendations for action on projects submitted to the commission by the states. The commission's internal structure is summarized in figure 2-2.

Commission Operations and Processes

An organization chart cannot convey the process by which the commission operates. For example, it cannot indicate the fact that the states, and the commission itself frequently meet in informal sessions in which issues are clarified and differences compromised. Equally, it cannot indicate the extent to which the executive committee discusses and narrows issues of policy which are subject to formal commission ratification.

Policy ideas, problems, and recommendations come to the commission table from many sources. They can come from the federal co-chairman and his staff, from the states' regional representative and his staff, from the executive director and the commission staff, or they can be brought to the table by any of the member states. The most usual pattern, however, is a staff presentation sent out with the agenda in advance of the meeting.

Allocations and Budget

One of the most crucial policy matters that the commission faces is the question of how it distributes its funds. At the time of the enactment, there was a general congressional intent that the commission give each state a sufficient share of the funds under each program to enable it to participate meaningfully in the program. Moreover, if each state viewed itself as competing with the other states for project funds, the result would have been a complete breakdown of operations or excessive log rolling. To avoid this competition, the commission decided to use a set of state allocation formulas for most sections of the act. These were developed by the staff soon after the commission started operation[7] and were recommended to the commission for adoption. They were adopted without amendment and the same allocation formulas have been used to determine the states' shares of the funds appropriated by Congress since 1965. Following the 1970 census, they were revised solely to reflect the data available from that source.

These allocations are not guarantees or, strictly speaking, block grants. They are better construed as reservations of funds that provide assurance to the states that if they follow through on their responsibility under the act, and develop acceptable plans and projects, that at least that much money will be available to

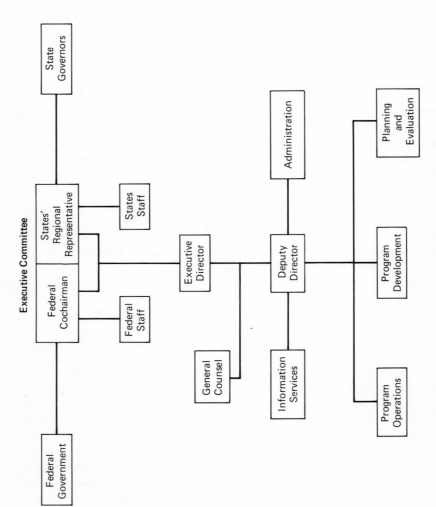

Figure 2–2. Appalachian Regional Commission Staff Structure.

them. States may, if they wish, trade funds from one grant type to another among themselves and frequently the commission staff serves as broker in these "swaps."

The annual budget for program funds is a federal instrument. It is included in the budget of the Executive Office of the President. The commission, through the federal co-chairman, receives budgeting guidelines from the Office of Management and Budget, and develops a draft budget. It presents this document to the Office of Management and Budget, which holds hearings and "marks it up," i.e., makes changes in the budget presented. The budget is then redrafted by the commission staff for inclusion in the president's budget documents presented to the Congress.

The administrative budget is a different matter since the administrative funds of the commission are paid half by the states and half by the federal government. This budget is jointly developed in detail and all staff and administrative expenses are approved by the commission. Each state's share of the administrative funds is determined by an allocation formula similar to the ones used to distribute federal program funds among the states.

State Development Planning

The commission requires each of the states to submit a development plan each year that provides the basic framework for activities under the program. The plan is to include statements of the state's goals and objectives for Appalachian development, its analysis of potentials for development, an analysis of area problems, a description of the state's proposed program plans for the coming fiscal year, and other longer-range analyses. The Appalachian state representatives have the basic responsibility for developing the plan for each state. Sometimes this is done by their own staff or other state planning units and in some cases the states have used consultants to develop the plans. The commission staff provides technical assistance to the states in helping them develop the plans. When the development plans are submitted to the commission they are first routed through the staff for review. A staff recommendation is then developed for the executive director to send to the executive committee, recommending whether the plans should be approved or suggesting that certain modifications in the plan be requested. The executive director then routes the plan to the executive committee members. Negotiation with a state frequently occurs in the process, leading to revisions in the plan or statements of expectations about future plans.

The Development and Approval of Project Packages

After the development plan is approved, the state proceeds to put together a project package appendix to the development plan. The project package specifies the individual projects the state intends to request during the coming year (although they are not applications at this point). The relationship between the project and the state plan is also described in the project package. It is at this point that the state must do considerable liaison work between any federal agency offices involved in the funding of projects and with the localities and state agencies that are involved. This project package is also given a staff review and sent to the executive committee for action in the same manner as the state plan.

Project Processing

Once the plan and project package are approved, project processing becomes rather straightforward, although by no means is it an easy matter in every case. Many of the difficulties in processing commission projects can be traced to the need to secure approval from some federal agency of their share of the project's cost prior to the time that the commission's official approval can be executed. The projects are reviewed by the staff of the program Operations Division with technical assistance from the other staff units when this is necessary. Once the staff decides the project is in proper form, and frequently after contact with the state and locality, it prepares an approval recommendation for the executive director to send to the executive committee. In practice, the commission does not reject a project. Because of the prior review of the project packages, virtually all submitted projects meet ARC criteria but may not meet federal agency criteria. In this case (if adjustment of the project is impossible) it is suggested to the state that the project be withdrawn. Out of approximately 2400 projects submitted, about 100 have been withdrawn.

Project Administration after Approval

For every commission program except the Section 302 research, demonstration and local development district activities, some federal agency has been named in the act to be responsible for project administration after approval. This was done to avoid the necessity of creating an elaborate commission staff for project administration since in many cases the commission grant is for projects already receiving a grant from an existing federal agency. After approval of a project, the necessary papers are prepared to transfer the funds from the commission's treasury account to the treasury accounts of the federal agencies involved. The federal agencies are then responsible for the usual technical and administrative review that is necessary to implement an approved project.

Extension of the 1965 Act

When Congress acted in 1965, it scheduled the demise of the commission for June 30, 1971. In these six years of operations, the commission engaged in highly diverse activities, many of which could not be expected to show effects in this period of time. Some, like early childhood programs, have effects whose magnitudes will probably never be fully discernible even when they begin to yield impacts. Others, such as the highway program, have discernible impacts now but have other aspects whose impacts are less obvious and may be more remote in time.

The commission's fundamental task was to initiate a process of change, one that required working with multitudes of public and private agencies and stimulating the creation of new ones. The building of public and private institutions and their stimulation are slow processes and with a limited life the commission itself could only be a temporary assistant to the region. Internal organizations and institutions with greater expected longevity have the principal role of stimulators and shepherds of the growth and development of the region.

As the six years drew to an end, there was unanimity in the commission, and strong Congressional and regional support for an extension of the effort for four additional years. Though phrased in more guarded terms, there was general recognition that the early ambitious estimates of what could be done in six years had been overly optimistic and, at least in the minds of some both in and out of the commission, the end of the initial six year authorization had originally been conceived as the date for renewal, not demise.

Coincidental with the desire to extend the act, President Nixon proposed revenue sharing with its revamping of federal-state fiscal relations. Part of his special revenue sharing plan for rural areas involved allowing the special Appalachian effort to disappear. Resounding opposition to this from the governors and from Congress produced a four year extension bill to which was attached a nationwide public works program addressed to the problem of unemployment. This bill was vetoed on June 29, one day before the Appalachian Act expired, but the president let it be known that he now supported the Appalachian program "100 percent." After operating briefly under temporary continuing authority, the Act was extended on August 5, 1971.

Vigorous support by the governors was predictable. The Appalachian approach gives them direct control over federal funds with far fewer restrictions than are customary with such monies and without having to appeal to their legislatures for appropriations (except for their modest share of commission and states' office expenses). Support in the Congress that led to an 88-2 vote in the Senate, for example, in support of the bill ultimately signed, was less predictable. Some might take it to be a sign of a well-conceived program, competently administered, that was doing its job. Such a conclusion would not be fully warranted, though partially true. The chapters to follow are designed to provide a basis for judging the degree to which virtually unanimous Senate support was warranted. It is not premature to note, however, that the senatorial judgment was a relative one—relative to the soundness, competency and effectiveness of the alternatives conceived or observed.

3 Past Policies and the Appalachian Condition

Concern for the performance of the regions of the country, and for obtaining their potential contribution to the nation, has been a consistent element of American national policy from its beginning. Repeatedly, Congress has enacted legislation, such as the Homestead Act and the land, timber and mineral grants and other subsidies to the railroads, that were designed to promote the economic utilization and integration of parts of the continent. From the very first Congress, there was concern expressed for the "opening of the West," and there is a certain irony in the fact that Appalachia is the focus of the latest large-scale regional development attempt. Appalachia was the first "West" that national policy tried to "open." That early attempt placed central emphasis on the opening of highway access, the National Pike, that ran west from Cumberland, Maryland. Today there is an Appalachian Development Highway that goes west from that point. Albert Gallatin, Jefferson's Secretary of the Treasury, proposed a series of highways and canals to open the mountainous heartland of Appalachia to development, and periodically through our history, Appalachia has had its problems discussed, its potentials explored, and programs for its development proposed. In this century, President Theodore Roosevelt transmitted a report to Congress dealing exclusively with Appalachia; TVA was (and is) a massive attempt to upgrade the region and its contribution to the nation; and in the 1930's, Benton McKaye produced a proposed program for Appalachia which is remarkably similar to the proposals implemented 30 years later.[1]

Of course, in all this attention, there was no agreement on where the boundaries of Appalachia lay. All agreed that the more rugged mountains of the center of the region in Kentucky, Tennessee, Virginia and West Virginia, were the heart of the problem. In addition to the physical isolation that they produce, mountains produce a psychological isolation that has been a resource and a restraint on personal achievement for those native to the area.

The present effort to assist the region flows out of all earlier activities and it is therefore impossible to precisely date its origin. As is so often the case, a combination of events, personalities, ideas, and fortuitous happenings occurred to precipitate the new interest and the absence of any one of them might have been sufficient to abort the effects of all the others. Individual preferences would give ascendency to one or another of these factors but, regardless of their ranking, some understanding of them is needed because each left its imprint on the attempt now underway.

One root of the present effort can be found in the battle between Senators

Kennedy and Humphrey for West Virginia's votes at the 1960 Democratic convention. Those who had later contact with President Kennedy, as he was persuaded to initiate special activities for the region, assert that his receptivity to the idea was largely a product of his shock at seeing at close range the miserable conditions in which some fellow citizens existed. The shocking contrast between his personal background and theirs may have importantly affected the trend of public policy.

During roughly the same period, the plight of parts of Appalachia was made evident to many other Americans. The early 1960's were the years when America was startled into seeing its poor. These were the years of Harrington's *The Other America* and similar sources of cultural shock. Appalachia had its publicists too. Harry Caudill produced a moving, angry illuminator in *Night Comes to the Cumberlands*, followed by others making similar points and also by a CBS TV documentary "Christmas in Appalachia" and by word and picture stories in such then popular magazines as *Saturday Evening Post*.

In all of these stimulators of popular understanding and sympathy for Appalachians, the concentration was on the most rugged and depressed central part of the region. The history and problems of that part of the region came to be identified as typical of all of it. Regardless of the accuracy, for example, of Caudill's account of the repeated rape of the people, land, timber and minerals of eastern Kentucky and the dispersed pattern of isolated living that exists there, both the problems and programs needed there are far different from those for Pittsburgh or Chattanooga, also parts of the region. The public's mental pictures of the region and its problems created a constraint (among many others) on the recommendations for ameliorative action.

Eastern Kentucky provided more than the pictures that were the occasion for the present program's initiation. In a circuitous way, it also precipitated gubernatorial approaches to President Kennedy. That area was hit by a particularly destructive flood in 1957. A rehabilitation study was undertaken that produced a far more sweeping idea than the usual catalog of desirable acts to ease the effects of the disaster. The basic points it made were that the fundamental problems of the area were beyond the ability of the localities or the state to remedy, that these problems were not unique to eastern Kentucky but were shared by neighboring areas, and that a regional approach to them was essential. By 1960, Millard Tawes was governor of Maryland and had on his staff a former member of the Kentucky government who remembered the recommendation for a regional approach. When Governor Tawes was faced with requests for assistance from the three western counties of his state, it was suggested that he respond by promising to call a meeting of Appalachian governors to seek a regional approach to their concerns. In May 1960, he called together the first meeting of what was then known as the Conference (now Council) of Appalachian Governors. Preceding the meeting, Maryland had prepared a consultant's report that defined the problems of the region in terms that have become familiar to many now but were known to the residents then—problems of access, employment, education, health, and migration. Eight of the present 13 Appalachian states were represented at the conference and joined in a proposal to all the 1960 presidential candidates that a regional approach be taken to the area's problems.

This petition for federal help was an admission of impotence to solve their problems using state and local resources and an expression of dissatisfaction with the results of prior national legislation to ease the burdens of distress. The assumptions and characteristics of those national programs, and the evaluation of their relative utility, were among the influential factors affecting the characteristics of any new program. An examination of them is necessary, therefore, for an understanding of the choices made in framing the program ultimately adopted.

Prior Public Policy

Prior to the 1930's, the dominant federal economic development activities had been expansionary. There was a continent and all its resources to exploit; opportunities and endowments were apparently limitless. If resources were poorly utilized and income inequality fostered, those were the seemingly minor costs of a wealth generating mechanism. For 50 years before the 1930's, rumbles of discontent and disaffection were heard in the Granger and Conservation movements, for example, and remedial steps were undertaken in the regulation of commerce, resource exploitation, conditions of labor, monetary affairs and monopolies, and the "adjustment" of agricultural markets. By hindsight, these can be seen as harbingers of the passing of an era but the dominance of expansionist ways of thinking effectively ended with the Great Depression. The frontier supposedly closed in 1890 but "frontier thinking" maintained a longevity far outstripping its objective rationale, an ideological lag of the type from which we continue to suffer.

The policy of the 1930's was addressed to a different set of issues. Economic distress could no longer easily be associated with personal inadequacies. It was the economy that was sick and the prescription was a pragmatically determined blend of monetary and fiscal policies, public works expenditures, manpower and resource conservation and development, and public welfare. World War II, and the preparations for it, obscure a test of the efficacy of all these efforts but a seemingly continually congenial medication was a part of the prescription. Repeatedly in the years since, and as recently as the present Congress, whenever economic distress occurs in an area or nationwide, public works are a proposed ingredient of alleviation. This fits well into our biases. Idle hands do the devil's work; to be useful, efforts should show tangible results; "things" solve problems. Public works efforts have produced highly useful public facilities, and continue to do so, but the technological basis for using them as aids to the unemployed has been seriously diminished. In the intervening 40 years, the unskilled labor component of public construction has diminished to the vanishing point and nowadays, the unemployed benefit more indirectly, than they do directly from employment on such projects as the additional income is spent and re-spent.[2]

Uncertainty about the effectiveness of the New Deal programs, determination not to slip back into depression, and enthusiasm that the monetary and fiscal tools elaborated in the intervening years would be effective, all combined to give the years immediately after World War II a different flavor. At the national level, its most important and tastiest fruit was the Employment Act of 1946 with its commitment to national programs to stimulate maximum employment. At the local level, the optimism of wartime prosperity was tempered by recollections of the distress of the 1930's and painful evidences of its return to selected areas. New England, for example, suffered prolonged distress as it felt the first massive industrial relocation of the post-war years.

Optimism, recollection and painful contemporary example produced a burst of local booster activities to insure that "it can't happen here." Multitudinous local organizations appeared of the chamber of commerce type, competing for the relatively few new plant locations by extolling local virtues and by promising direct and indirect subsidies from local and state sources. With so many communities seeking so few manufacturing plants, inevitably the stakes went up and only gradually did communities begin to sense that success might be illusory. The subsidies extracted could approximate the benefits the community might experience, though not those to the direct employees. Local and state costs for industrial bonds, shell buildings, and loan guarantees, combined with tax abatements or reductions to leave "successful" communities precariously advantaged. The years brought examples of communities saddled with shell buildings that were never occupied or that were deserted when the employer moved on as soon as the period of subsidy was exhausted. Footloose industries, paying low wages to female employees were the typical "catch" of the depressed older communities and of some of the areas in transition from an agricultural economy.

Elements of the belief that the way to economic salvation is through a committee of local boosters persists, and the belief may not be totally erroneous in individual cases. However, when conducted by many, many communities it can hardly be the basis for national policy. Booster and subsidy efforts by communities are mutually offsetting, the number of prospects are too slim, and the probability of success without a relatively rare combination of public facilities and markets is too low. Through the 1950's, those areas most likely to lose out in the competitive scramble came to be identified as "depressed areas" and special national legislation to assist them gradually evolved.

The senior sponsor of the several "depressed area" bills of the later 1950's was Senator Paul Douglas of Illinois. The first of these, introduced in July 1955, reflected his awareness that manufacturing areas were in particular trouble and he therefore proposed loans to communities and to new or expanding industries, rapid tax amortization as an attractive lure, and manpower training and financial assistance to unemployed workers. The response to this first depressed areas bill, which passed the Senate and never reached the House floor, set much of the pattern for the later attempts to legislate in this manner in that era. First, the bill was progressively amended to include areas of more varied economic structure. Specifically, rural and agricultural areas were granted potential benefits in the effort to marshall sufficient votes to obtain passage. Secondly, the bill encountered opposition from the Eisenhower administration which persisted in the view that depressed areas were a local problem. As a concession to pressure, it had earlier proposed a small revolving fund to make loans to new or expanding businesses in these areas. As history shows, it was not prepared to go as far as the various Douglas bills since in both 1958 and 1960 depressed area bills received a presidential veto. Both times, the stated reasons for rejection centered on the fact that grants to local areas could reach 100% of costs, that criteria for eligibility were vague, and that too many areas would qualify. Other reasons were also offered but the basic reason for rejection was philosophical. The administration did not believe local, concentrated unemployment was of major national concern.

The Area Redevelopment Act

Areas of concentrated unemployment, and particularly West Virginia, were important political battlegrounds in 1960. Kennedy had promised West Virginians that if he was elected, he would send Congress a program that would bring jobs and industry to the state and to other "neglected areas." He had become a sponsor of the various Douglas bills and Senator Douglas was a logical choice to head the task force that was appointed immediately after the election. By January, 1961, its recommendation of a comprehensive program to aid depressed areas was ready and, not surprising, a key element was the rejected Douglas bill of the preceding year. With a change that housed the new program in the Department of Commerce, the proposal received administration support and on May 1, 1961 the Area Redevelopment Act was signed and the Area Redevelopment Administration was born with a legislated four year life.

Though it had other potentially important elements, particularly the provision of manpower training, the most notable aspect of the law was its authorization of almost $400 million in loans and grants to eligible areas for use in constructing public facilities. There were two basic requirements for eligibility—meeting the legislated criteria of persistent unemployment and underemployment and preparing an Overall Economic Development Program (OEDP). The geographic unit for eligibility was the county and the criteria were sufficiently loose to permit over 1,000 of the roughly 3,100 counties in the nation to qualify. About 20% of the national population lived in the eligible areas.

Problems of various types and dimensions plagued ARA's efforts. First, and perhaps most obviously, a comparison of funds available and areas eligible suggested the need for a priority ranking among eligible areas. The legislation provided no criteria for doing so and, in fact, rather than developing them internally, ARA became particularly sensitive to "inquiries" from Capitol Hill about the status of projects and hastened to approve those about which inquiries were made. Secondly, the OEDP became a hurdle to be surmounted to gain funds rather than a useful planning device. In too many cases, the OEDP's were prepared by consultants with little local involvement and with commentary that could easily have applied to numerous localities. Perhaps this is all that could be expected because of the geographic narrowness of the planning base. It is difficult to do perceptive analyses on a county-by-county basis since that approach does not encourage recognition of wider area dependencies and interrelationships.

The belief underlying ARA's legislation was that what stood between a depressed area and prosperity was the need for a plan and for public works. The latter proved in many cases to be water and sewer systems. ARA took its mission to be a stimulator of job creation and it consequently assumed that its expenditures were the vital final causative event when new jobs appeared. It regularly and immodestly calculated the cost of new jobs created. This outlook spurred it to a "bird-in-hand" approach that responded to claims or opportunities of increased manufacturing or recreation employment without regard to the existence of other opportunities or of fundamental inhibitions to basic improvement in an area's fortunes.

ARA's problems were compounded as the years passed. In 1962, a far more attractive program of manpower training was instituted nationwide, leaving ARA eligible areas without special manpower training incentives to potential locators. The following year, a $9 million Accelerated Public Works Act (APW) was given to it to administer. APW allowed more areas to participate, about 150, with more than 10% of the national population. It was an emergency action, designed to overcome the intractable problem of unemployment. Administration of APW further compounded the growing impression of widely dispersed activities funded by ARA, some of questionable value, lacking a consistent strategy within each area and certainly among areas. Moreover, the program always lived with the fears of the Congressional representatives of more prosperous areas, namely that the depressed areas would lure away the industrial citizens of their areas. Always present also were those who questioned the widsom of depressed area legislation at all, those who contended that it was an interference with the processes of economic readjustment and that because of that interference, a price of lost efficiency was likely to be paid. Critics could point out that the amount of direct employment of the unemployed on public works was insignificant; that the number of areas eligible (combined with the funds available) meant a scatter-shot approach that had little impact on any area; that it was unrealistic to assume that every depressed area could be rejuvenated; that far more than facility improvements were needed to upgrade the skills and health of the adult population and properly prepare the youth of these areas; that the planning stimulated was too narrow in geographic and programmatic focus; and that the states were by-passed even though their authority and investment for economic and social development in these areas far outstripped those of ARA.

The Grant-in-Aid Approach

As disillusionment with the operations of ARA and APW grew, so did the awareness that the whole structure of federal-state relationships was going awry. At the present time, a manifestation of this awareness is the suggestion of block grants, or revenue sharing, with the states. A competitive response to the problem is the regional commission-regionalism approach that has Appalachia as its prime example. Both approaches are grounded in a belief that the grant-in-aid approach as it grew from the 1930's to 1960's is not satisfactory.[3]

During these 30 years, the number of grant-in-aid programs has mushroomed, as have the funds disbursed to local and state governments under them. In the mid-sixties, it was estimated that there were over 1,000 such programs, each with its own requirements. They had all been created to solve individual problems in separate functional areas and the early ones had fairly simple procedural mechanisms. As they increased in number, however, more complex requirements and procedures were established, and more specific planning requirements were attached, as policymakers attempted to organize the growing system. In fact, however, it was not a system. It was not designed to make available a coordinated set of federal aid programs to assist states and local governments. Rather it was a collection of separate programs characterized by overlaps, duplication, gaps, lack of coordination and even direct conflicts (see Chapter 9).

Those with a working knowledge of the collection of grant-in-aid programs recognized that proliferating sets of one-to-one relationships developed between federal agencies and their state and local counterparts that shortcircuited attempts by higher level executive leadership to achieve coordination. For example, an attempt by a governor to exert control over a program in his state could precipitate an informal advisory to their parallel federal counterparts by the state bureaucrats who were resisting "intrusion." The "Feds," comfortable with their existing constituency relationships, would respond with a ruling or an advisory that changes in the state's procedures would threaten the continued availability of funds. Throughout the federal-state system, functional subgovernments arose that were relatively immune from executive control because, at the federal level, it was possible to protect the federal bureaucrats from unwanted "intrusion" through the pressure that could be developed.

Other complaints arose. Although there were several agencies offering assistance of similar types, there were important areas in which no programs existed. When more than one federal program was needed so that a combined local program could be instituted, synchronization was virtually impossible to obtain. Requirements differed, the authority of federal field staffs differed, the field staffs were uncoordinated. Most programs required planning but they were for differently defined geographic units with different planning requirements so that a plan prepared for one agency was unlikely to satisfy any other. Moreover, though planning was required, if it was to have any impact it should have been designed to help allocate funds but the availability of funds depended upon the vagaries of congressional and agency procedures. Knowledge of the funds to be available rarely was in hand as state and local governments established their own budgets. A final, and fundamental complaint, was that the availability of federal funds for specific purposes induced appropriation of state and local funds for those purposes whether or not they were high priority needs.

From the standpoint of the Appalachian governors, the years immediately after 1960 had not produced programs that were having a beneficial impact on the problems of their states. They argued that the proliferating grant-in-aid programs were straining state and local budgets, were making their jobs as chief state administrators more difficult, and did not permit or promote a concerted attack on the pressing issues. They had been promised that ARA would be beneficial but they had their doubts about this also. As the president had promised, a special office had been established within ARA for the purpose of assisting the region. Its existence had helped to keep the Conference of Appalachian Governors alive, though it would probably have lived anyway, and it had served as a vehicle for getting matters of special concern expressed. It is unclear whether or not it had any particular effect on the flow of project funds into the region. Under both ARA and APW, the eligible areas in the region received a proportion of the total funds available about equal to their share of the total population of all eligible areas. Whether or not the region was receiving the share of funds to which (in some sense) it was entitled, the governors were not impressed by the results. There was apparent consensus that some projects were poorly planned at the local level, that the program was diffuse and uncoordinated, and that it was inadequately attuned to the financial and program needs of the region.

The Presidential Commission

The president had made his promise of a special office within ARA to the governors at a meeting in May 1961, one week after ARA was born. This undoubtedly would not have been a propitious time to espouse a special Appalachian effort but by April of 1963, the situation had changed. Two years' experience with ARA was in hand and again, nature had dealt another blow. The spring of that year brought devastating floods. On April 9, when the president and governors met, the Conference of Appalachian Governors (CAG) sought emergency assistance for the heartland of the region and a joint federal-state commission to plan a comprehensive program for the region. The president agreed to both. He set in motion machinery that produced the 1963 emergency relief effort and he established the President's Appalachian Regional Commission (PARC).

The structure of PARC reflected the joint nature of the approach the governors had recommended. Under the federal chairmanship of Franklin D. Roosevelt, Junior, the Undersecretary of Commerce, PARC's executive secretary was John D. Whisman, the organizational mainspring of CAG and of its eastern Kentucky origins. The executive director of the staff effort, and ultimately a dominant force in the entire undertaking, John L. Sweeney, came from the staff of the Senate Committee on Education and Labor. A miniscule staff, supplemented by University of Pittsburgh researchers, served the year-long PARC effort.

The commission organized subject matter teams and sub-teams that were also jointly federal and state.[4] They were instructed to make assessments and recommendations in their specified areas. Simultaneously, PARC was taking formal and informal "soundings" of sentiments, experiences, desires, prohibitions and resistances in the private and public sectors, and at all levels of government. In combination, these studies and "soundings" provided the information base for the series of compromises and accommodations that characterize group decision-making. By a series of progressively refined approximations, the widest possible range of understandings and interests were served. The process of accommodation was not perfect, as can be seen in the dissenting views of the governor of Pennsylvania included at the front of the final report, but a rather diverse group of interests were accommodated.

This early process of agreement was facilitated by the lack of a predetermined maximum sum that could be sought. That issue was ultimately faced and resolved when state and federal interests agreed on the authorizations to be sought in the draft bill submitted to Congress. The accommodative abilities of the parties, or more accurately their awareness that too vigorous disagreements might mean that everyone would get nothing, was put to a test following the assassination of President Kennedy. Though President Johnson indicated his support for the joint planning effort, his 1964 State of the Union address incorporated, as parts of his War on Poverty, priority programs that had been planned for inclusion in PARC's report. This required alterations of priorities within the report and further accommodations by those who had advocated a lesser emphasis on facility construction programs. They had to be content with the anticipation that Appalachia would be receiving needed health, education and welfare services from the newly proposed national programs. Experience shows that any misgivings that were felt at the time about the likelihood of successful cooperation with these new programs were justified.

By coincidence that was not accidental, the PARC report[5] was delivered to President Johnson on April 9, 1964, exactly one year after the establishment of PARC by President Kennedy. It presented a description, diagnosis and prescription for a region whose boundaries had only been determined in the course of the PARC deliberations, a region consisting of counties in ten states, not the present 13. Even within the ten, shifts in boundaries have occurred in the intervening years.

With such impermanent boundaries, what makes Appalachia a region? Are the characteristics of the included counties such that as the boundary is crossed, the statistical and topographic indicators will unambiguously report that a different region has been entered? The answer to this is no. Despite this, the PARC report's assertion that "Appalachia is a region apart" is true—but only on the average. On the average, Appalachia's counties share the characteristics PARC ascribed to them but on the periphery, they are not notably different from their excluded neighbors.

The boundaries of the region were not determined by any one person or by any one system. Beyond general agreement that included counties should be those that were relatively mountainous and relatively poor, the drawing of the boundary in each state was largely a state decision in which unspecified factors and unspecified weights were applied. The incorporation of counties to widen Congressional support by including one from an additional Congressman's district was not only acceptable, but desirable. Factors of local and state history and politics played their part as well. The development strategy to be followed in the program was less influential in setting boundaries than the presence of problems typical of the included areas. This development strategy only evolved after important boundary decisions were made. The result was that important areas, neighboring areas of growth potential, were omitted from the region. Some neighboring areas that were impoverished in some states were excluded while less impoverished areas in others were included. Overall, Appalachia was defined as the common backyard of the Eastern and Midwest-Mississippi Valley industrial zones of the country. Subjecting the regional boundary determination as originally formulated and later amended to an ultimate pragmatic test, however, shows that it was adequately designed. It produced sufficient support both in and out of Congress to be declared a region entitled to preferential treatment.

Despite the lack of clear statistical and topographic determinants of its borders, Appalachia has certain common economic characteristics.[6] Historically, there have been four main legs of the Appalachian economy—agriculture, railroads, mining, and primary manufacturing. Appalachia's economic base was heavily concentrated in the very sectors of industrial activity that have had declining employment for several decades. This is the common source of many of the region's problems.

Although rich in resources, the economy of parts of Appalachia has concentrated on their extraction, rather than processing, at the time when shifting markets and changing technology dramatically reduced employment in agriculture and mining. In common with extractive-based economies throughout the world which have exported resources for processing elsewhere, economic returns have been relatively sparse.

Many Appalachian communities, from small towns to metropolitan areas, still rely on one or two dominant industries. Such economies are highly sensitive to technological and policy shifts and business cycles. Appalachia is filled with farm market towns that no longer have any markets, mining towns that are ill-equipped to compete for anything but a share of the remaining employment in mining, and mill towns that have lost their once valuable locational advantages and are unable to compete effectively for other kinds of economic activity. This led PARC to assert that "rural Appalachia is lagging behind rural America and urban Appalachia is lagging behind urban America."

To a very large extent, then, the Appalachian Region has been the victim of technological change. Changes in technology are, of course, a national phenomenon. The changes advancing technology have wrought are not peculiar to Appalachia alone. Many parts of the nation are able to respond to these new conditions, however. They have reached a stage of diversity in their development that enables them to attract and develop new forms of economic activity to replace the old. But regions such as Appalachia have lacked the intellectual, social, and economic capital necessary to provide this kind of adaptability.

The President's Appalachian Regional Commission highlighted six major problems of the Region:

1. *Low Income*—One Appalachian family in three had an annual income of less than $3,000 compared to the national figure of one family in five. Less than nine percent of the Appalachian families had incomes of over $10,000 a year compared to nearly 16 percent for the remainder of the United States. Per capita income in Appalachia was $1,400 while the national figure was $1,900.

2. *High Unemployment*—While five percent of the U.S. labor force was out of work, over seven percent of the Appalachian labor was unemployed. PARC estimates indicated that in some counties of West Virginia the true figure may have been 30-40 percent unemployment.

3. *Lack of Urbanization*—While the nation was 66 percent urban in 1960, Appalachia was only 44 percent urban. Appalachia had and still has one of the highest concentrations of rural nonfarm population in the United States, reflecting the dispersed settlement patterns that accompany a resource-dependent economy. These dispersed populations are more difficult to reach with adequate public services.

4. *Deficits in Education*—In 1960, 42 out of 100 people in the United States

over age 25 had completed high school. In Appalachia the figure was only 32 out of 100. Similar patterns were found for dropout rates, college graduates, and literacy levels. All of these figures also masked unmeasurable differences, such as the quality of education programs.

5. *Deficits in Standards of Living*—The 1960 census revealed that the average Appalachian bought fewer services, fewer automobiles, and purchased less in the way of retail goods. His housing was of lower quality and lower value than the national average. Over 34 percent of the housing in Appalachia was deteriorating or dilapidated compared with 23 percent in similar condition in the remainder of the United States.

6. *Changing Population*—Those most able to leave the region in search of new economic opportunities were the young working-age adults. They left behind older people with obsolete skills and the very young who were still in school. This phenomenon of a population that was relatively young and old provided a mounting picture of distress. It requires higher levels of public service and yet is less able to provide the tax resources necessary to finance them.

In summary, the region was found to be lagging behind the nation in a variety of critical dimensions—income, employment, employment structure, degree of urbanization, health, education, and public facility availability. The problem was seen in both economic and social dimensions, overlaid with an awareness of the extent to which isolation was a pervading condition. Ending that isolation and other public remedial actions was the underlying theme to assure greater participation and contribution to the nation from the region.

The PARC report detailed what it called the four normal steps in the development of a region that was rich in resources:[7]

a. The exploitation of natural resources produces local wealth.
b. That local wealth is invested in human and social capital or community facilities (such as housing, education, transportation, public and private services, hospitals, planning commissions and the like).
c. These investments provide a platform for an upward spiraling development process. That is wholly independent of the original natural resource base of the region.
d. Sustained progress is dependent upon continued development of human and social resources originally attracted to the region by the natural resources.

PARC emphasized that this pattern did not occur in Appalachia. The wealth from exploiting natural resources left the region. Investments in the community economy and social system were never made. Thus, the stage was never properly set for a spiraling process of regional growth.

This then, was the primary case for the Appalachian regional development program. The lack of community facilities and social services was the continuing cause of the region's decline. These gaps must be overcome in order to reverse the downward slide and bring about a process of development.

PARC visualized a program of highly interrelated public investments in highways and facilities, such as hospitals, schools and other community facilities, that would both upgrade the human resources of the region and attract economic growth and diversification. These would be combined with investments to increase the productivity and regional benefits from natural resources. Overseeing all of this would be a new set of institutions at the regional and local levels that would carry out the development program and strengthen the ability of the public and private sector to foster a desirable future for the region.

The recommendations submitted by PARC were attempts to remedy the defects of public policy in the past (and particularly those of ARA), to blend insights from analysis with considerations of practicality and feasibility, and to initiate a new organizational approach to social and economic problems. In Chapter 5, the specific recommendations are examined and the alterations and refinements that occurred during the process of legislative review and administrative implementation are indicated. However, at this point it is important to note that the PARC report is relatively silent on issues of strategy. For example, it places no emphasis on the differences in program requirements that might exist between an emerging Georgia factory community and an obsolescent West Virginia mining community of equal population. It gives no insight into how the approach to development would differ in Pittsburgh, an old metropolitan area, from the appropriate combination of programs for Huntsville, Alabama, an emerging one. Establishment of a basic strategy for the regional development effort occurred largely after the submission of the PARC report. Those strategic decisions were a blend of apparent political feasibility and of the understanding of the development process that theory could offer. The next chapter summarizes the state of regional development theory as it existed then and indicates the strategic options that flowed from it.

4

Conceptual Bases of an Appalachian Program

Fundamental to an understanding of how public policy is formed is a grasp of the range of alternatives available for consideration. A host of factors help determine that range. Some stem from prior experience, such as those outlined in the preceding chapter. Some arise from the political environment. What cynics derisively called "politics" can be more productively viewed as the cultural and institutional boundaries on what it is practical to consider. Still other determinants of the range of alternatives arise from our intellectual understanding, from our theory of the social process to be affected. In combination, these all help determine what is thinkable and what it is practical to think and undertake. A principal role for any adviser is to refine the theory, i.e., to perfect the range of what is thinkable, while helping to extend the range of thoughts that are practically useful. The economist brings to this task a heritage, frequently a melange, of theories and concepts which are the basis of his disciplinary contribution to public policy decisions.

To be useful for this purpose, a theory of regional economic development must highlight the crucial factors which influence the dynamic process of change and explain their interaction. To a significant extent, these theories are grounded on observation. Their common objective and common basis in observation makes their differences largely ones of degree. The dichotomy suggested by separate names and discussion tends to mask their similarities.

No matter which theoretical approach to understanding regional economic performance is adopted, all agree that regional economies are part of a national economy whose fortunes dramatically affect regional prospects. The theorizing and uncertainties about the national economy which are current when a regional program is created therefore inevitably, and properly, leave their impact on that program.

Regions and the National Economy

In the late 1950's and early 1960's, academic and policy debates occurred concerning the nature and causes of the continuing unsatisfactory performance of the American economy. Unemployment levels were high and, to compound matters, recoveries from recessions were too brief and insufficient to absorb those seeking work in the labor market. Fears were expressed that automation was destroying jobs at a faster rate than new opportunities were appearing.

33

Suggestions were current that controls on labor displacing technology might be required or that substantial alterations in the customary duration of the work week, or working life, might be needed.

In this environment, two opposing schools of thought contested for acceptance as the basis for public policy. One group argued that the national problem was caused by a deficiency of total demand. To them, the prescription followed from the diagnosis. The national policy announced in the Employment Act of 1946, achieving maximum employment, they said called for a series of acts to close the "deflationary gap." Policies of fiscal deficits and monetary policies to increase the availability of credit and decrease its cost were urged. This would increase aggregate or total demand, and would lead to the creation of new jobs and allow relatively easy adjustment to the displacements that technological advance necessarily entails.

An opposing group agreed with the premise that sufficient total demand was a necessary condition for amelioration but it argued this would not be enough. They were impressed by the observation that nationally unsatisfactory performance had an unequal impact on parts of the nation and adopted a structuralist point of view. They saw a problem in the rapid obsolescence of industries and firms and skills that an aggregative approach alone could not solve. They wondered if the areas which had borne the brunt of the unemployment would be the focus of the recovery and decided probably not. Those taking this approach, emphasizing the structure of the economy, believed they saw areas of distress that were unable to compete for new opportunities, that would continue a slow process of decline in a generally affluent nation, and whose residents would be required to go through a slow, painful process of relocation as the geographic distribution of population adjusted to opportunities. During that process, personal losses would occur but so would social losses as the economy found itself with labor resources that were geographically unavailable for the jobs that the aggregative approach might stimulate into existence.

The issues were made more complex by the awareness that developed in the fifties that part of the economy's response to expansionary aggregative policies may take undesirable forms. A "trade-off" was perceived between unemployment and inflation. As national policies to overcome excessive unemployment have their impact, the response to increased demand may be higher wages and prices rather than greater employment and output. Increased demand may be expressed in a decreased value of money rather than an increased real value of output. It was said that this arose from a lack of the classical form of competition that expects available unused labor and output capacity to thwart price-raising desires. A host of institutions, of which labor unions and dominating corporations were only the obvious examples, were said to have achieved insulation from the competitive forces that were supposed to dampen their price and wage raising desires.

An economy that had become inflation-prone in this way presented serious obstacles to an aggregative policy of overcoming unemployment by increasing total demand. Areas of high unemployment are not likely to initially feel sufficient impact from remedial policies to have their unemployment absorbed. Their persistent unemployment will appear in the national statistics, leading to further remedial steps. These will continue to have impact on areas whose unemployment has already fallen to the level at which prices and wages start to rise. These increases occur and begin to spread as each increase provides the rationalization for others. Ultimately, the dilemma of rising wages and prices accompanying unacceptable levels of unemployment appears, requiring a choice, or compromise, among unsatisfactory alternatives.

In this setting, those who supported a structuralist approach could offer an additional policy alternative. They began with the view that immobility of both labor and capital will continue to leave some of these resources in lagging regions idle except possibly in periods of extremely rapid expansion. Therefore attempts to reduce the national level of unemployment using total demand approaches will be stymied when that unemployment is largely concentrated in lagging areas. The alternative course suggested was to focus policy attention on these areas themselves. This would have a dual impact on the inflation-unemployment dilemma. First, its intended effect was to reduce unemployment directly. Second, it would make additional output available to the economy which would have a price and wage dampening effect. Overall, the structuralists argued that their approach would make it possible to simultaneously aid the lagging areas and move the national economy closer to achieving the twin goals of maximum employment and price stability.[1]

Two considerations moderated enthusiasm for this policy. First, as discussed in Chapter 3, attempts at fostering area recovery had not borne promising fruit. The pragmatic question asked was whether national policies could affect regional performance. The second consideration asked the more fundamental question of whether we should even try to affect regional performance and, if we should, are there some policy approaches that have different implications than others.

The basic economic reason offered for rejecting a policy designed to alter regional performance was the need to make efficient use of our available resources. Unemployment, and particularly persistent unemployment, is an evidence of an inefficient waste of resources. When that unemployment is geographically concentrated, efficient resource utilization requires that labor and capital migrate to the opportunities where efficient utilization can occur. Resource mobility, therefore, is necessary for economic efficiency. A policy that restricts or retards mobility is therefore to be condemned on economic efficiency grounds. Aid to lagging areas was said to fall into this category because it would retard mobility. Other grounds for rejecting it were also offered.

It is often assumed that economic activity occurs at the most efficient location, i.e., at that location where the costs incurred by the producer are at a minimum. A policy of aiding depressed regions could lead producers to locate where costs were not at a minimum and society would be forced to pay higher costs to attain the same quantity of output. This was offered as another efficiency reducing effect of an area assistance or regional development program.

Taking efficiency as the objective of national policy, it was argued that area assistance should be avoided. It reduces the mobility of resources toward their best use and distorts the geographic distribution of economic activity.

This conclusion was contested however. Some objected to using economic efficiency as the sole criterion of policy. They argued that other goals—income redistribution, avoiding the personal and social costs of mobility, preserving the rural-urban balance of the population and the associated social values, avoiding problems of excessive population concentration—were also important. However, those who contested in this vein implicitly accepted the conclusion that an area assistance program leads to inefficiency. It is true that (fortunately) we have other national objectives besides efficiency. But it was also not clear that efficiency losses are inherent in an area assistance program since even in its absence, federal, state and local governments affect private decisions about suitable locations for economic activity.

Public acts and inaction are a fundamental influence on what are the privately efficient locations. Everything from transportation, to taxes, to utility rates and availability, to labor force quality, to market availability are influenced by government policy. It is artificial therefore to think of government as being neutral in its impact on area economic performance. Consciously or (usually) unconsciously, government is deciding where, as well as what, is going to be within the feasible range for private decisions. Government's prior decisions have established the range of locational alternatives now available to the private sector of the economy. It was argued that a policy of area assistance could be viewed as comparable in its impact to policies we have always had. It simply makes area impact a conscious part of our policy. However, it also raises questions about the ways in which that policy should attempt to affect the private sector.

There are two extremes to the spectrum of alternative means of influencing private decisions, with shadings between them infinitely possible. The first is an extension of the past. Government has helped establish the range of locational alternatives and in doing so, has contributed to leaving some areas non-competitive. When new locations for activity are considered, these areas are quickly eliminated in the cost-conscious calculations of the businessman. To assist an area, the economic environment of the area could be changed. Changing its locational attributes through transportation improvements, the health, education and attitudes of its people and the public facilities it offers will enable it to be an efficient location for new employment. Advocates of this approach suggested, in effect, that employers in these areas be provided with a subsidy of social and economic public capital availability comparable to the subsidy of the same type now available elsewhere. A policy of this type associated lagging regional performance with an insufficient ability to provide the public capital that employers need to keep their costs from being relatively higher than those elsewhere.

At the other extreme of the policy spectrum, the same recognition of higher costs leads to the suggestion of direct subsidization or "assistance" to firms to help them offset them. Though Congress has frequently provided direct subsidy to businesses, it likes to think of these cases as exceptional and historically it has preferred the indirect approach, i.e., altering the range of efficient alternatives among which firms may choose.

There may be good reasons for this. Direct subsidy cannot distinguish between the internal inefficiency of the firm and the external inefficiency of its location. Area assistance policies are designed to offset the latter but not the former. The hope is that lagging areas can become suitable hosts to competitive firms and thereafter, in the long run, require no special augmentation of the inducement to locate in them. A program of direct subsidy falters when a subsidized firm responds to the termination or reduction of aid with the threat to retire from business. The indirect approach avoids this but at a cost.

The cost is the uncertainty about which changes in the economic environment are critical to raising the probable success of the area in the cost-competition for new jobs. This uncertainty has profound implications for the operations of a regional development strategy, as later pages of this book will relate.

As PARC set about choosing its recommended strategy, the national economic policy debates were still in process and were very pertinent to its task. They seemed to suggest the following considerations that needed to be borne in mind as potential insights from regional economic development theory were explored. From a national point of view, a policy of regional development:

1. requires a high level of national demand;
2. may assist in harmonizing goals of maximum employment and stable prices;
3. does not necessarily result in efficiency losses of output;
4. may serve national goals other than efficiency;
5. requires that awareness of the impact on areas become a more conscious part of governmental policy; and
6. avoids direct subsidization of employment only at a cost of increased uncertainty about the appropriate acts to take.

Export Base Theory

One basic approach to an understanding of regional economic development borrows heavily from the concepts of international trade. Its basic thesis is that to sustain a viable economy, a region must export. The ability to sell "abroad," i.e., outside its boundaries, is the economic basis for a region's existence. Deplete or eliminate this competitive ability to sell and the non-export sectors of the regional economy will also decline. Increase "foreign" sales and the non-export sectors will grow. The name "export base theory" aptly describes the concept.

Both intuitively and descriptively, the export base theory has a certain appeal. It accords well with our personal experiences—if we do not sell to others, we cannot buy—and with a capitalist ethic. It meshes easily with an emphasis on exports that we retain from the mercantilist period, when merchants were the dominant economic class and persuaded society that its welfare required sending foreigners useful goods of greater value than were received in return. It also conforms to some of the teachings of another early group of economists, the Physiocrats, who convinced themselves, and others, that productive activity resulted only in the production of material things, agricultural products. There is an easy identification of exports with physical products. There can therefore be an almost thoughtless acceptance of exports as "basic," as region-builders, and of output for local consumption (what is frequently labeled "services") as "non-basic," as region-filling. Moreover, history is replete with cases of communities that were built on an ability to export, that then lost their physical or economically competitive ability to do so and declined. Their experience appears to support the forecast of the theory.

Upon reflection, nagging second thoughts arise. First, taking the world as a whole, except for some extra-terrestrial garbage, we do not export. To accept an export base theory means arguing—and proving—that what is true for the parts is not true for the whole. A convincing case for this has yet to be made. Secondly, history is also replete with cases of communities and areas that lost their export base and continued as reasonably successful economies. The local-serving sectors of the economy were the persistent ones, as new exports were substituted for the old. It becomes reasonable to ask, which are the basic sectors of such an economy, the enduring or the transitory ones? And third, reflection raises questions about the ready identification of exports with commodities. Nevada has long prospered on exports of gambling services and marital rearrangements and a mainstay of New York City's economy is the financial services it provides.

Myriad attempts have been made to calculate the statistical counterparts of the export base theory. In fact, one of the attractions of the theory is the ease with which it can be converted into a statistically operational model. The economy is divided into its basic and non-basic sectors. Their ratio is calculated and the resulting factor or "multiplier" is used to estimate the importance of the export sector and the overall impact that changes in exports would have on the area's economy. A multiplier of three would mean that for each new export job created, two additional service jobs would appear.

These procedural steps are sometimes taken at great cost and with meticulous care. Other times, quick calculations "on the back of an envelope" are all that are done—or required. Common to all, however, are several problems. First, repeated tests have shown that the size of the resulting multiplier is dependent on the number of categories into which the area's economy is divided, and the geographic extent of the area studied. Generally speaking the larger the area studied, the larger the multiplier. Secondly, the multiplier only measures the average ratio between exports and services. This is not necessarily the ratio of effects that would result from a small charge in exports. And third, a multiplier that is based upon employment data is not necessarily the same as one based on the amount of income generated by the export and service industries.

However, the fundamental export base hypothesis is evident in all applications. The flow of causation is assumed to run from exports to services and there is no way to directly incorporate the reverse flow, i.e., from a service sector which is able to provide a range of economically supportive inputs that induce the growth of export-oriented industries. Overall, the export base theory gives dominant emphasis to external demand and it gives scant attention to cost factors which are fundamental to supply considerations. This theory also provides no means to easily analyze the opportunities that so-called "import substitution" create. These opportunities to expand an area's economic activity arise when it produces internally goods and services which it formerly obtained from outside.[2]

Despite its one-sided orientation toward external demand, the export base approach retains its appeal and is widely used. In areas that have a relatively undiversified economy or which have no unusual supply and cost advantages or disadvantages, some of the severest problems can be minimized. It is true, in all probability, that for any region of a national economy, external sales of goods and services are a (not *the*) fundamental determinant of present and future activity. The degree of importance of this determinant undoubtedly decreases as the economic size of the region grows relative to that of the nation. Particularly as a conceptual tool, as distinct from its statistical uses, export base theory has value. By focusing on the competitive ability to sell, it emphasizes a fundamental factor in a market economy. It has the additional virtues of relative simplicity and intuitive appeal. For economically small areas, it may be a sufficient basis for understanding.

If the theory is applied to Appalachia as a whole, however, it does not yield sufficient insights. Appalachia has historically supplied the nation—and much of the world—with coal, lumber, iron, steel and heavy equipment. When these sales boomed, times were good, just as the theory would forecast. As sales, and more importantly, as the labor component of sales declined, so did overall activity, as the theory would suggest. But the theory shed no light on important questions.

If the goal is regional recovery, the theory says export more. Unanswered is what to export, to where, from where in the region. Also unanswered was why were declining exports not counterbalanced by new ones, as experienced in other areas. Was Appalachia unique? What did it have in common with other unfortunate areas and in what ways was it unique? What role was being played by its location, by its population distribution, by its natural resources, the structure of costs employers faced? Moreover, the economy of the region remained heavily export-oriented despite the declines. How should it capitalize on this? Are exports the help the theory suggests or are they a hindrance? Why is the internal economic structure of the region different from that of the nation, or is it? What are the implications of this structure for the future of the regional economy?

Export base theory urged finding new exports to sustain the region. In the past, the instability of export industries had been the apparent source of repetitious cycles of distress. Even if the basic lesson of the theory were accepted, i.e., to prosper-export, the region appeared to require some protection from an unmitigated repetition of that cycle. For this purpose, the theory could suggest only diversification of exports to "spread the risk."

Public policy formulation needed more insight than export base could offer, more than the counsel to look beyond the region's economic borders for its sales and salvation.

Stages Theory

With notable exceptions,[3] export base theory is applied in a static manner, looking at the economy at one moment of time. A related, but quite distinct alternative approach adopts a more dynamic, sequential view of the process of regional economic development. This stages or sectoral theory of regional growth is an adaptation of an approach that has been widely used to explain the process of development of national economies.

An historical sequence of events is hypothesized. The economy of an area originally develops around a primary activity—agricultural or extractive—that provides an exportable surplus over local needs. The proceeds from these sales provide the means for acquiring imports of items not produced locally, typically manufactured goods. Gradually, the size of the area market grows sufficiently to make it feasible to produce locally some items that were formerly imported, import substitution production. In turn, the volume of this output gradually grows and attains sufficient efficiency to permit the export of these former imports. Then more sophisticated capital goods and other supplies are produced internally. Eventually, the area produces a well-diversified range of secondary (manufacturing) output. By this period, the relative importance of the original export basis of the economy has been severely reduced. The area has embarked on a process of self-generative growth that ultimately takes it to a stage of tertiary industry dominance. Now service, i.e., non-goods producing, industries are of major relative importance as sources of employment and in total, exports play a relatively insignificant role in the area's economic life.

This stages theory of development also has an intuitive and historical appeal.

Americans, in particular, may find that a responsive chord is struck. A fur-trading post on the Columbia River is recalled that evolved into a metropolitan region. The theory seems to fit the example. In fact, the theory appears to accord well with our entire economic history. Probably, if the stages theory had an easily applicable statistical counterpart, it would challenge export base theory in the frequency of empirical applications.

For all its attractiveness, however, the stages theory must be assessed as being more descriptive than analytical, and its descriptive generality is suspect. In fact, all areas do not pass through the series of stages hypothesized. Some begin the sequence as it is visualized, make progress and then stagnate, cases of arrested development. Others make similar beginnings, progress and then return to an earlier stage, cases of retrograde development. Still others skip stages and never experience the sequence visualized, cases of precocious development. Clearly, depending on the geographic definition of the region adopted and the number of phases within each stage that is considered, exceptions more numerous than examples can be found.

To claim that a theory is not fully descriptive is not a fundamental indictment, however. The function of a theory is to illuminate critical causal connections. The analytical adequacy of a theory is the more important test. The desire for an analytical understanding of the development process arises because so much of the orientation in regional economics, as in much of the entire discipline, is toward projecting the future course of an economy and assessing the impact of alternative policies on it. A theory has weathered an important test, though not been proved valid, when the future conditions it anticipates occur following the adoption of specified policies.

Stages theory does not provide that degree of understanding. Its basic strength lies in its emphasis on the evolutionary character of a regional economy but it provides meager insight into the conditions that are necessary and sufficient for the completion of the entire process. Emphasis on economies of large scale production, on the size of market, import substitution and related matters is helpful. These are concepts useful for an understanding of the growth process, even though not presently precisely quantifiable. Full analytical utility, however, requires an understanding of the differences between those economies that "make it" and those that do not; of the conditions that produce retardation and retrogression; of the processes at work in the precocious economies; of the relationship between regions, as well as conditions in them; of the influential role of the early character of industry, ownership, income distribution, and social and demographic characteristics. At present, we have bits and pieces of information and impressions that all these, and more, leave their impression on the evolutionary process but no melding into a more general stages theory has yet occurred. Nor may it ever, since there is no certainty that the stages approach will be the basis for the analytical insight into the process of regional development that we desire.

At present, this approach can help clarify the basis for some policy decisions. It can assert with reasonable assurance that some economies are too small or weak or remote or debilitated to generate the economies of large scale production and concentration of activity crucial to the complete evolutionary process. At the other extreme, it can confirm that some economies, large metropolitan ones in particular, have reached a tertiary, self-generative level that makes significant absolute declines unlikely. But most areas and regions and subregions and communities fall between these extremes. Full utility for public policy purposes requires posing the policy alternatives for them and positing the probable results. It requires, ultimately, providing a basis for the decision that some specified acts, done in this particular place are worth doing while other actions there, or similar ones elsewhere, are not. The unspecified variables, their magnitudes and relationships are too numerous for that precise a prescriptive projection.

Turning again to the case of Appalachia, the PARC report makes specific reference to the stages theory.[4] It provided the norm of typical progression toward a dominantly service oriented economy against which the region's retarded and retrograde development was contrasted. This was followed by the explanation that the region's poor performance was due to its historic inability to invest sufficiently in its people and social infrastructure of transportation, public facilities and the like. Though a possible diagnosis stemming from the stages approach, that theory does not provide a strong basis for asserting that greater investments in the future would lead the region to resume its evolutionary march through successive stages.

The PARC report's reliance on the stages theory, however, does highlight another useful emphasis of this approach. In contrast to export base theory, the stages theory provides for an examination of the costs borne by producers, and of opportunities for local-serving industries. It can therefore stimulate a fuller evaluation of a region's prospects and can lead, as in this case it did, to an emphasis on internal factors. In an important, though perhaps unconscious way, it provided a basis for turning thinking about policy alternatives inward, onto the region, rather than outward, onto its markets, as export base theory would have done. Rather than counseling external sales as the route to remedy, the counsel was toward internal improvement.

Balanced and Unbalanced Growth

Though quite different, the two preceding approaches to an understanding of regional economic development are built around the relations among industries. In the case of export base, it is a one way relationship, from the export industries to the service industries. In stages theory, the relationship has greater reciprocity, local-serving industries growing along with local markets until they attain competitive export ability and then inducing the development of supply-ing industries. However, neither of these theories treats the reciprocal relation-ships of industries and markets in quite the way that characterizes the advocates of balanced or unbalanced growth.

It may seem strange to begin a discussion of two such opposite sounding approaches with an emphasis on their similarity but, in fact, there is a common view between them. Also, both are subject to the same differences in interpreta-tion. Balance, or unbalance, can have either an industrial or a geographic definition.

For present purposes, it is sufficient to trace the beginning of the balanced growth doctrine to World War II and concern for the post-war development of Eastern Europe. In simplest terms, the argument presented builds upon the commonsensical notion that the world economy consists of each of us doing the other's wash. In more precise terms, the argument stated that it would be feasible in an underdeveloped area to build a range of manufacturing industries but not any one singly. The income generated by a shoe factory, for example, would be allocated by its workers to many types of products, not simply shoes. An adequate total demand for shoes would depend upon income being generated in the production of a variety of other goods whose workers would also spend their income on a diversity of products. The balanced creation of industry was therefore essential for successful development.

This thesis provided a means of measuring balance, as well as a rationale for seeking it as a goal. The appropriate measure of balance was the relative growth of various industries in proportion to the demand for their products as incomes rose. Other versions of this thesis appeared, implying other measures of balance, such as the preservation of the ratio of prices or the relative values of foreign exchange rates, but they all have common aspects. All look to the phased development of industries in a symbiotic relationship to each other. All would apparently require a well articulated planning mechanism or, at least, a means of communication and assurance to private entrepreneurs that would enable them to incorporate in their calculations the intentions of others.[5] All focus their attention on the demand side of the market and implicitly assume no supply constraints. They emphasize demand as the limiting factor whose constraints are the principal impediment to development. These can be surmounted by balanced elaboration of the economic structure. Leads or lags in any sector would undermine the dynamism for progress of all.

Advocates of unbalanced growth as an approach to economic development would probably agree that at the end of the process of economic evolution, in the probably not-so-happy stationary state, output and demands should be in balance. The parting of the ways occurs basically on the initial assumption that demand constraints are controlling. Born largely out of experience with non-European attempts at development, unbalanced growth emphasizes critical supply constraints. The most pointedly announced are of public and private managerial and entrepreneurial ability. The scarcity of these talents is said to inhibit development and means must therefore be found to economize on them. Unbalance is the suggested answer.

In summary, the argument for unbalance distinguishes between autonomous and induced actions. Autonomous acts do not follow logically from easily observed conditions and require a large component of the scarce talents. Induced acts do not require as much managerial and entrepreneurial ability since the need for them is generally obvious following the impacts which autonomous acts may have. Progress toward development can be accelerated if scarce talents are used to undertake acts that have a high induced followership. An appropriate strategy of development is one in which manifest enticements to induced behavior are always present. An example might be building a highway without bothering about provision for maintenance. If it is used and requires upkeep, pressure from users will induce maintenance without consuming scarce planning abilities in advance. This public-private example could have other counterparts in which, for instance, the appearance of a new firm in an area induces the appearance there of its suppliers or customers or of consumer goods suppliers to its employees.

The emphasis in the unbalanced growth approach is on making certain pivotal decisions, those with a high ratio of induced to autonomous acts. In many respects, it is similar to the theory of a market economy, which depends on signals through the price and profit mechanism to induce businesses to capitalize on opportunities. The difference, however, is that there are no counterpart price and profit signals to measure the ratio of induced to autonomous acts. The pivotal acts to make must be deduced from study and understanding of the economy of concern. Balanced growth provides for more measurable guides to policy.

Given the institutional setting in which the Appalachian program was created and the region's intimate economic relations with the entire country, a program based on the balanced growth thesis was unthinkable. Its requirement of a considerable amount of guidance to economic processes was too far from accepted approaches, even if technically feasible and programmatically desirable. Moreover, since it is an integral part of the U.S. economy, such an approach to solving the region's problems would have required information about and guidance to activities well beyond its borders. Neither regional nor national policy makers would have viewed recommendations based on this approach as either practical or desirable. If balance was sought at all, it was in the far different sense of achieving parity with the rest of the nation in social and economic terms, per capita income and education, for example.

The approach adopted for Appalachia shows much more affinity for the unbalanced growth thesis, though with significantly different terminology and with emphasis on a different type of scarcity. There was agreement that growth could be encouraged by creating conditions that would induce the desired private decisions that lead to the creation of jobs. The scarcities that were the impediments to growth had to be overcome. However, these were not principally ones of managerial and entrepreneurial talent, though the region could certainly have used more of this too. Rather, the scarcities were found in health, education, public facilities and access. Remedying these, it was argued, would create opportunities that would induce growth. The unbalanced growth idea had evolved in underdeveloped countries. Translating it into the context of a relatively underdeveloped region of a developed country altered it fundamentally. One essential remained, the concept of altering the economic landscape to induce entrepreneurial and managerial acts.

Location Theory

Among the roots of the theories of the development of regional economies is a body of location theory that attempts to understand the locational decisions which determine the geographic or spatial structure of society. The essential questions asked concern the factors considered by locators and the weights given to them; the economics of tendencies to concentrate and disperse spatially; the relationship of concentrations to each other; and the spatial structure unique or appropriate to each stage of economic development.

This last point, which gives a spatial dimension to the stages theory, is of particular importance. If there is a certain geographic distribution of economic activity that is conducive to further elaboration of an economy, then public acts could be directed to fostering it rather than, perhaps unwittingly, retarding it.

In the most popular formulation of this theory, a plain devoted exclusively to agriculture is assumed. Hypothetical events occur and the spatial rearrangement associated with later stages of development are described and analyzed. In the earliest stage, all segments of the plain are like all others. As the economy evolves specialization takes place which, as it elaborates into a modern economy, produces centers of economic concentration, the urban places of contemporary society. Many reasons are given for the appearance of towns and cities—transportation, markets, economies of large scale production, economies of concentration, nonmarket economies external to the firm—which up to some limit enable particularly favored locations to become metropolises.

The concept builders seek to understand the relationships among these cities and towns and from their inquiries the idea a system or hierarchy of cities has appeared. This system is built on the supposition that there is a balance in the sizes and functions of urban places that is dictated by their relations to each other. Special functions unique to each higher level in the hierarchy have been hypothesized and empirical evidence sought. The distance and size relationships among cities has been measured and generalized. In sum, a body of central place theory has been created based on the concept of a balanced spatial system of urban places, each type of city with specialized functions. Central place theory is consistent with stages theory. The latter visualizes economic evolution leading to a predominantly tertiary industry, or service, economy. And the production and delivery of services has historically been largely an urban function.

It might be agreed that economic specialization leads to urbanization and that urban places tend to develop in a symmetrically balanced pattern but that agreement would provide a meager basis for identifying policy alternatives. This would be true in general but is particularly true in the case of Appalachia whose population was more rural, and non-farm rural, than the rest of the country. If the urban structure-central place skein of analysis was to be productive, it would have to lead to a better understanding of the relationship between urban places and their surrounding rural areas, their hinterlands.

Two sets of influences flow between the more developed part of a region, its towns and cities, and its less developed rural areas. First, there is a polarizing effect that draws capital, labor and population, and other resources to the center. This effect, taken by itself, tends to drain the hinterland to satisfy the needs of the center through a relationship that is similar to the one between a colony and its imperial ruler. The result might be a decline in the dollar value of per capita income in the hinterland but, more likely, per capita income relative to that in the cities falls as the bearers of rural investments in health and education migrate. If the rural area has had a relative surplus of labor, then dollar incomes might even rise. However, overall, the polarizing effect tends to diminish opportunities for development in the hinterland by reducing both resources and markets.

A reverse effect, a spillover effect, also exists between a center and its surrounding area. This takes many forms. The most frequent and obvious is the export of income from the center in the pockets of hinterland residents who commute in for work and the export of urban services to hinterland residents. Less obvious is the flow of private transfer payments, gifts and support payments, that are sent back home by immigrants. Particularly in the case of larger centers, a dominant spillover can be the outflow of manufacturing and commercial enterprises seeking the markets of the hinterland and avoiding the congestion and other diseconomies of the centers.

However, when the centers are small or sufficiently remote from their hinterlands, spillover effects do not provide a compensating flow for the polarizing effect rural areas experience. They continue to provide human, capital and material resources to the centers but do not acquire the full range of spillover effects, missing particularly the availability of urban services, the acquisition of commuters' incomes, and the importation of decentralizing industry.

This situation came to be viewed as the nub of Appalachia's problem. Contained within the statement of the problem is an obvious potential solution—stimulate the creation or growth of centers in the hinterlands and the enlargement of existing centers, so that their fields of influence, their spillover effects, would leave less and less of the region feeling only the effects of polarization.

Growth Poles

A growing body of regional development doctrine supported this idea. An important antecedent was the idea of growth poles which, as originally formulated, were not places at all. Rather they were firms or industries whose growth spread through the structure of industry to stimulate others at dispersed locations. The region associated with these poles was the enterprises on which the force of growth impinged. An easy, perhaps too easy, translation of this growth pole concept into geographic terms occurred. The pole became a center, a city, whose growth impinged upon its hinterland, ameliorating conditions there.

This idea permitted several strands to be woven together. A growth center could be visualized as a community within a hierarchy of urban places whose export base allowed it to grow and progress to later stages of development. It would be an increasingly stable, geographically expanding provider of employment, urban services, and other opportunities to its hinterland. Ideally a symbiotic relationship would exist, with polarizing and spillover effects working to the mutual advantage of all.

This was the model that underlies the strategy chosen for the Appalachian effort. The terminology selected emphasized the area to be affected and the phrase "growth area" became the common expression.

Acceptance of this growth area approach provided for less than complete guidance to answers for such problems as identifying potential centers, or forecasting the size, function and hinterlands of existing and new centers, of selecting and implementing public actions likely to stimulate and encourage the development of these centers.

Also absent was guidance to answers to questions about the appropriate public policy toward areas without existing or potential centers and far from the field of influence of those others.

General guidance was provided by the model accepted. The concept had to be elaborated and refined in application, it had to be expressed in a strategy for the development of the region.

5 Strategies for Appalachian Development [1]

The task faced by PARC was to blend diverse considerations into a regional program. Influences were exerted by the region's condition, the policies and programs of the past, PARC's judgment of the political feasibility of alternatives, and insights from theory. As indicated at the end of Chapter 3, PARC's stipulation of a recommended strategy was incomplete. The strategy it began to define was further refined in the process of securing legislative sanction, and refinement is still occurring as experience adds to the understanding that can be mustered for perfecting it. In fact, one of the main threads that runs through this chapter and the entire book is the path of that evolution and the reasoning that motivated it.[2] A strategy, after all, is a unique combination of separate programs that is designed to take advantage of their interaction. Changing the relative emphasis among programs is therefore a change in strategy, as is a change in the types of programs employed.

PARC's Recommended Strategy

PARC rejected a regional strategy based on a policy of accommodation. Such a policy would accept continuation of the trends of the recent past with only the hope that their personal impacts could be mitigated. It implies no attempt to alter fundamentally the evolving geographic distribution of national economic activity among regions. The associated trends of population out-migration would be regarded as a necessary adjustment process and there would be no conscious attempt to create new migration or commutation destinations within the region.

PARC chose instead to develop a strategy based upon a policy of growth inducement that would operate on the assumption that the recent trends, which were the reflection of myriad private decisions, could be changed. It believed that underlying these trends were numerous government decisions about investments and public facility availability and that altering the pattern of these public decisions could affect the direction of the trends.

PARC believed that public decisions, made in the light of the evolving national trends in industry growth and carried out at the right time and location, were capable of creating new geographic alternatives within the region for firms to consider. It anticipated that improving the region's competitive position would lead to economic growth and that this, in turn, would lead to general development, the enlargement of the range of social opportunities available to

49

the region's residents. The clearly implied theme of the PARC report was that economic growth, i.e., enlargement of income-earning opportunities, would lead to this more general development, a belief that was far more readily accepted in the early 1960's than a decade later.

The policy of growth inducement recommended by the President's Commission relied upon the example of many underdeveloped countries which were using public investments to try to stimulate private capital investment. It recommended the translation of these foreign aid principles into a domestic program. Since that time, there has been much discussion of the extent to which public activities in underdeveloped countries have been successful in inducing private activity and whether this is the most efficient strategy to follow. Although there is still uncertainty about the efficacy of this approach in the developing countries, their experience was not and is not precisely applicable to a case like Appalachia. In this country, the focus of policy is on a relatively depressed region of a developed economy. The competitive alternatives available to newly locating firms are far more numerous than in an underdeveloped country. However, there is also a far larger number of firms making location decisions. The parallelism between the case of Appalachia and that of the underdeveloped countries may not be close and foreign experience may not be fully instructive.[3]

A second strategic assumption by the President's Commission concerned the evolving urban and industrial pattern in the United States and its implications for Appalachia. Data from preceding decades and estimates of developments after 1960, as well as information from other sources, strongly suggested that the areas in and around the country's larger cities would be the homes and work places of increasing percentages of the population. Industrial data clearly suggested that the noncommodity producing sectors of the American economy were the probable creators of a majority of the new jobs of the future. In summary, these inquiries forecast an urban, service industry employment and residential structure.

Implicit in the report of the President's Commission was the assumption that if Appalachia was to obtain a greater share of national output, it would have to adjust to the evolving trend of the national society. Consequently, its strategy was designed to assist the region to alter both its residential and occupational pattern to one similar to that of the country so that it could find a fulfilling role in the national scene.

The full significance of another implication of the urbanizing, service employment trends was only gradually grasped. If manufacturing was going to provide a decreasing proportion of national employment, then all communities could probably not hope to attract manufacturing plants. The attraction of manufacturing might be an effective strategy at selected locations, but was far less likely to be fruitful as an overall strategy. The President's Commission made no recommendations for new federal inducements to industrial location. It did recommend that the states continue, and consider expanding, their programs for providing industrial credit. However, this emphasis on state activity was not primarily a reflection of the probable scarcity of new manufacturing location opportunities. Rather it reflected the intense competitiveness for manufacturing prospects among the states. A regional program of direct industrial attraction which would have had to settle interstate rivalries potentially faced a seemingly impossible task.

Post-PARC Evolution of Strategy

Once a strategy of growth stimulation through public investments was recommended, it was still necessary to define more precisely the character and location of the investments to be made. The PARC report, as previously mentioned, noted a relative lack of urbanization as a deterrent to Appalachia's development. The report also cited the then recent relative improvement in service employment in Appalachia as a hopeful sign that readjustment to the evolving national pattern was beginning. However, the report did not draw these various strands together. Only during the year that elapsed between the presentation of the PARC report in April, 1964 and the enactment of the legislation did a unique regional strategy crystallize. A strategy based on concentration of investments in growth areas was adopted. It is expressed in one critical sentence of Section 2 of the act which instructs that "public investment . . . shall be concentrated in areas where there is a significant potential for future growth, and where the expected return on the public dollars invested would be the greatest."

As implemented, the strategy has placed more and more emphasis on the role of urban places as locations from which public services are delivered and has tried to emphasize the creation of area-serving capabilities in them. At the same time, it was anticipated that there would be a gradual migration of people from the more remote areas toward these urban places, analogous to the exodus which occurred from those hollows that did not receive electric service to those that did. In summary, implementation of an area-serving urban strategy was attempted.

Three factors were at work that lead to the policy prescription of Section 2. The first was dissatisfaction with the results of a policy of dispersal, the basis of ARA's increasingly criticized operations. The second was the growing weight of conceptual support for a program that capitalized on the advantages thought to lead to growth in urban centers. Third, and the culminating factor, was an awareness that the magnitude of the job to be done in Appalachia precluded the likely availability of sufficient funds to engage in development activities in every community and area of the region. Budgetary restraints therefore counseled selective, concentrated efforts.

Adoption of this strategy raised questions as well as answered them. Immediately pressing were the three questions of a) who will pick the "areas with significant potential for future growth," b) who would decide which investments were to be made, and c) to what extent would comparisons of growth potential between states be made.

In the months preceding passage of the act, but after submission of the PARC report, it was firmly decided by the states and federal officials that the states would have the responsibility for picking these growth potential areas, subject to review by the new commission based upon criteria mutually acceptable to them and the federal government. However, the development of these criteria was left to the post-enactment days. An intimately related decision was that the states would make project recommendations. They were not to send on all requests received but were to exercise primary responsibility for rejecting unsuitable proposals on the basis of criteria that were also unspecified at the time.[4]

Also in these intervening months, a first attempt was made to identify the locations of economic growth which existed in the region. This study made clear that in Appalachia, as was true nationally, the principal centers of growth were the major cities. A strategic dilemma was apparent. The most depressed areas of the region, those in which poverty and deprivation demanded the most remedial actions, were the same areas that could not, on historical evidence, be viewed as the likeliest locations of future economic promise. For program purposes, this dilemma was resolved by establishing growth potential as a relative condition and allowing each state to designate those areas within its part of the region which seemed most likely to be the future centers of employment, population and service delivery. In effect, the growth area strategy was applied as a regional principle. However, only within each state were relative rankings required. Intraregional, interstate comparisons were not made. To do so would have bypassed precisely those areas of the region which, in the mind of the public, were the prime examples of the reasons for the program's inauguration.

The policy that evolved is an attempt to compromise the differences between an economic efficiency-oriented program and a social welfare-oriented program. The former would have led to focusing all activities on the prime prospects for growth, the widely separated larger cities. The latter would have emphasized programs leading to direct income enhancement, wherever people were located. The compromise was designed to result in a wider dispersion of job creating centers than would have been fostered solely by an efficiency-oriented approach but not to dissipate all available funds on areas that had little future prospects or on programs promising only short run income enhancement.

Adoption of the growth area strategy raises questions about the boundaries of the region that were established in this period. Surrounding Appalachia as defined in the law are a series of metropolitan areas which are the likely focus of development for nearby areas within the region. The exclusion of Cincinnati, Nashville, Atlanta, Charlotte, Roanoke, Harrisburg, and similar cities would be illogical if the region had been defined solely on the basis of a growth area strategy. However, this was not the sole criterion for regional delination. In both the state capitals and in the federal government, administrative and political factors also required consideration. Some states were highly conservative in selecting areas for inclusion. Virginia, for example, applied topographic and low income criteria so restrictively that only 21 counties were recommended for inclusion. Had the more generous criteria of a state like Pennsylvania been applied, far more of Virginia could have been included in Appalachia. In fact, had these neighboring cities plus larger areas of states like Virginia been included within the region, application of the formulas used by the commission to allocate its appropriated funds to the states would have resulted in grossly different proportionate distributions. Other allocation formulas obviously could have been established but in all probability, inclusion of densely populated areas would have resulted in lesser allocations to the states in the central part of the region where the problems of unemployment and distress were most prevalent. There had to be a compromise between a region that was too small to marshall political support and one so large that central Appalachia would not be a major proportion of it.

In practice, exclusion of these major centers has proved to be less of a problem than might be expected. In planning its program, the commission has made investments which were designed to improve linkages between areas of the region and their nearby external major cities. This is certainly true of the development highway network which links parts of the region more closely to these cities in time-distance terms. It is also true of the vocational education program, for example. As the commission's interest in the instruction offered in the schools it supports has increased, it has emphasized the likely availability of jobs in surrounding areas, which include these external, peripheral centers.

The Expression of Strategy in Programs

Just as the general strategy of an Appalachian program was refined in the months following the submission of the PARC report, so were the specific program recommendations. PARC identified four priority goals requiring significant investments:

a. Providing access both to and within the region.
b. Utilizing the region's natural resources of coal, timber, and tillable land.
c. Utilizing the region's rainfall and water resources.
d. Improving the education and health of the people.

Generally speaking, PARC's specific recommendations can be divided into two general categories—those that were expansions or accelerations of existing federal programs and those that marked new departures in general federal policy.[5] It recommended expansion and acceleration of existing programs in the following fields:

- a $1.2 billion highway program to link Appalachia with the major metropolitan markets lying just outside the region.
- a $36 million program of accelerated water resource facility construction.
- a broad range of conservation and resource development programs including pasture improvement, timber business development, power studies, minerals utilization, and marketing. The report also encouraged construction of recreation areas already planned for the Region.
- a program of action in the federal human resource agencies to meet the region's needs for improved education, especially vocational education, employment and welfare services, nutrition, and housing. Specific funding proposals were withheld pending action on the Administration's poverty program.
- a program of community development, based on an expansion of existing federal agency programs to encourage industrial expansion in lagging communities.

Beyond these programmatic recommendations, PARC proposed three innovations that distinguish its proposals and that give the present Appalachian effort some of its distinctive characteristics. The first was the establishment of a special fund for supplemental grants that would enable hard-pressed communities to participate in existing federal grant-in-aid programs. The supporting argument advanced was that Appalachian communities tended to be so poor that they were barred from full participation in existing programs by their inability to raise the full local share of the costs. Congress was asked to appropriate money without knowing which of the available grant-in-aid programs would be supplemented. To this extent, it was asked to relinquish some of the controls it can exercise through the appropriations mechanism.

The second innovation proposed was the establishment of a joint federal-state commission. Congress was asked to establish an agency in whose administrative costs the states would share. But more importantly, it would be an agency in which the federal government and the states would jointly make decisions on regional policy and on the allocation of funds appropriated by Congress. PARC was suggesting that the states collectively be given a role equivalent to that of the federal government in all matters of policy, program and expenditure that came before the agency. No rearrangement of powers quite like this had ever before been attempted within the federal system.

PARC's third innovative recommendation was also for a new governmental mechanism. It was an attempt to overcome the incapacities of small units of government. Not only were these units too small to plan effectively but their diminished fiscal resources had left them financially incapable. They could not participate financially in the programs that their situation required. The suggestion was that multi-county local development districts be created. These were to be the links between the states and local units of government and also between the public and private sectors. PARC recommended the creation of a regional development corporation. This was to be a mixed ownership, federally chartered corporation that would sell bonds to raise funds that would be used to implement the plans formulated by the local districts. Though not highly specific about the potential uses for these funds, PARC specifically mentioned that they were not to be used to provide capital for private industry. Of the three innovative proposals, only the development bank aspect of this last one did not survive the legislative process.

PARC's selection of program recommendations was based upon a belief that there was a limit to the acceptable number and scope of innovations that could be included in the initial regional program. Except as just indicated, reliance was put on the federal programs then in existence. This meant that the regional program was to be composed largely of those areas of activity in which the Congress had already enunciated federal interest by creating a program. The prospect of new federal programs for human resource development under the poverty program was coupled with an anticipation of coordination and cooperation with OEO. This left the new regional commission with its major activities largely in the areas of public facility construction, the creation of new organizations and the coordination of local, state and federal programs.

Following the President's Appalachian Regional Commission Report, the Johnson administration submitted a bill to Congress in 1964 that closely followed its recommendations. The Senate passed a version of the bill, but the House did not act. The bill, with some amendments, was then resubmitted in 1965, passed, and signed into law on March 9, 1965. As passed, the act also paralleled the PARC recommendations very closely. It authorized the supplemental grants, the federal-state decision-making mechanism, and the development district program. Thus, the act set up a dual experiment. First, it was an experiment in regional economic development designed to overcome the problems of Appalachia. Second, it was an experiment in federalism, designed to test new kinds of institutions in our governmental process. A new feature in the legislation, and one that gained perhaps more attention than any other aspect of the bill, was its specification of an investment strategy in Section 2 that has been commonly, but narrowly, known by the term "growth centers."

The program authorizations in the bill were all for two years (with the exception of the highway program) and provided:

- a six year authorization of $840 million to build up to 2,350 miles of development highways and up to 1,000 miles of access roads.
- $41 million for grants of up to 80 percent of the cost of building demonstration hospitals, diagnostic and treatment centers, and $28 million for operating cost grants which could go as high as 100 percent of the cost.
- $17 million for grants to help local landowners prevent erosion and to promote soil and water conservation.

— up to $5 million for loans to establish local timber development organizations.

— $36.5 million for eradicating mining scars such as extinguishing fires, filling mine voids, and rehabilitating strip mines.

— $16 million for grants for vocational schools under the Vocational Education Act.

— $6 million for grants for the construction of sewage treatment works under the Federal Water Pollution Control Act.

— $90 million to supplement other Federal grants-in-aid so that Appalachian communities could receive up to 80 percent of project cost from federal funds.

— $5.5 million for research and to defray 75% of the administrative expenses of local development districts.[6]

Since 1965, the basic structure of the Appalachian Act has remained unaltered. Within this structure, there have been important shifts in program emphasis, and of strategy, which will be discussed later in Chapters 5 and 7. Significant changes in the law have been made, however, some of which also reflect changes in strategy.

Administrative Changes:

1. The amendments of 1967 ended the original arrangement under which funds for Appalachia were appropriated to the secretary of commerce who released them on ARC's recommendation but following his own staff's review. (The full implications of this are recounted in the discussion of ARC-Economic Development Administration relationships.) Under the present procedure, funds are appropriated to the president and transferred to the federal co-chairman who releases them for disbursement upon ARC action. No longer are commission judgments about project suitability subject to federal agency review.

2. The 1965 act permitted the inclusion of counties from New York State into the region, a step soon taken by the state and ARC. The 1967 amendments added counties in Mississippi to the region. The 1969 amendments called for consideration of a further enlargement in New York State and New England but the region's boundaries have remained as established in 1967.

Program Changes:

1. In 1967, the commission's recommendation for a change in the health demonstration section (202) were accepted, allowing it to fund the operating deficits of facilities not built under the 202 program.

2. Also in 1967 and on the basis of ARC recommendation, the act was amended to create the housing development fund whose operations are described in Chapter 8.

3. In the same year, ARC was instructed to conduct a study of the impact of acid mine drainage throughout the region.

4. In 1969, Section 202 of the act was amended again on ARC recommendation, broadening its coverage to include nutrition and child development and occupational diseases related to coal mining. The financial assistance available in the program was liberalized.

5. Also on ARC recommendation, contract authority on highway projects was approved in 1969 which allows the states to obligate authorized funds more quickly than they were being appropriated. There have been frequent amendments to the highway section of the act which extend its legislative life, increase the funds authorized and add to the authorized mileage. These are detailed in Chapter 8.

6. The three year limitation on funding of local development districts was removed in 1969, providing longer term financial support.

7. In 1971, when the entire act was extended beyond its anticipated 6-year life, Congress allowed deficits incurred in the operation of vocational education programs to be covered from appropriated funds.

8. At the same time, authorization was given for the use of supplemental funds to augment the amount of basic Federal money available for programs in the region, rather than allowing the supplemental funds to be used only to augment local funds.

Guidelines for Program Implementation

Creation of a program for regional development is only partially completed when its general strategy has been established and authorization of specific activities has been granted. The next step is to determine how to apply the general strategy to those programs, i.e., to devise the guidelines for implementation. While taking this step, ARC felt impelled to show prompt action. It therefore began to approve projects while formulating more detailed operating guidelines and procedures. This "quick start" period was frankly undertaken for political and public relations purposes but was used to provide time to develop guidelines and understanding more in keeping with the general strategy adopted.

As the commission thought its way into the problem of establishing guidelines for program operation, five basic concepts influenced its thinking:

a. The commission had to attempt to understand the emerging patterns of economic development in the United States and, to the best of its ability, to work with them so that ultimately the region could develop the capacity to contribute more to national development and economic growth.

b. Substantial investment in human capital was required, not only because the people of the region were the commission's principal concern, but also because "without investments in the health and skills of the people, resources would remain inert and capital would never appear," as an early commission document put it.

c. The location of the region between the major metropolitan regions of the East and Midwest created the possibility of integrating much of the Appalachian economy with the national mainstream by strengthening transportation linkages with major nearby centers.

d. Development of a well-articulated economy required a growth strategy which recognized the relationship between urbanization and the potential for growth in a local area.

e. Public services and facilities were viewed as part of the necessary supporting infrastructure for most private investments in manufacturing plants and in services. The investment strategy would have to be attuned to that relationship and place highest priority on those public investments in each area most likely to foster the growth of the area economy.

These concepts all led to an emphasis on the role of urban places. They gave a notably urban emphasis to the prescription in the act to focus investment on "*areas* with significant potential for future growth." Those "areas" came to be identified as urban places because nationally, we were urbanizing and shifting our employment to service jobs in urban centers. If Appalachia was to capitalize on this trend, among other things, it had to strengthen selectively those urban centers, either existing or to be created, which could be judged on the basis of their performance, location, and potential to be most likely to grow. Appalachia's relatively underdeveloped urban system, existing or potential, came to be viewed as a competitive part of the national system of cities.

As the commission began its operations, two aspects of urban development were believed to be particularly important:

First, some minimum level of urbanization must exist if economic growth is to occur. In Appalachia there seemed to be too many places that did not reach this minimum level (whose exact magnitude was undefined) despite the existence of a large and dense rural non-farm population. In such areas urbanization, perhaps of unique character, might have to be induced. "New Towns" and functional partnerships among proximate small towns were the types of alternatives in mind.

The other characteristic of urban development which had to be taken into account was the tendency of urban centers, once they reach a certain size, to disperse into surrounding rural hinterlands. These forces or spillover effects, motivated by rising costs in the urban center, could offer an opportunity for Appalachia, particularly when these forces were pressing into the region from the outside. Whether originated in or outside the region, they provided one mechanism to distribute more widely the benefits of concentrated development.

The national setting was summarized in the ACIR study then being drafted.[7] It estimated that half of the population growth in the coming years was likely to occur in metropolitan areas of over one million persons, and that most of that growth would occur in the suburbs. Most of the remaining growth, that study projected, would occur in smaller-sized metropolitan areas. Towns below 10,000 in population, rural villages, and farms would have the lowest growth rate. Growth in small communities was expected to be uncertain in amount and duration.

After careful consideration, the commission concluded that its major emphasis should not be on the large metropolitan areas. In part, its efforts were an attempt to divert the flow of rural migrants away from such areas. On the other hand, the commission could not attempt to concentrate efforts in those communities whose location, topography, and other limitations made them least likely to respond to programs designed to increase economic growth.

In the very early months of commission operation not all these thoughts had fully crystallized. Enough was understood, however, to establish the general criteria that would guide the states in designating areas of investment focus. By resolution, the commission required "the identification of areas which, in the state's judgment, have a significant potential for future growth and other localities from which the population must be served in order to promote overall development of the Region."[8]

At the same time that it adopted this language, which was largely a repetition of the act, the commission adopted its "Policies for Appalachian Planning," designed to provide more precise guidance on the identification of "areas with a significant potential for future growth." The following paragraph provided a working definition of a growth center:

By a center or centers is meant a complex consisting of one or more communities or places which, taken together, provide or are likely to provide a range of cultural, social, employment, trade and service functions for itself and its associated hinterland. Though a center may not be fully developed to provide all these functions, it should provide or potentially provide some elements of each and presently provide a sufficient range and magnitude of these functions to be readily identifiable as the logical location for service to people in the surrounding hinterland.

The commission defined those "linkages" that should exist between the designated center and its hinterland. These include commutation patterns, wholesale trade services, educational and cultural services, professional services, inter-firm and inter-industry trade, governmental services, natural resource and topographic considerations, and transportation networks.

The policy statement then differentiated between primary and secondary centers by saying that classification as one or the other is dependent upon the range of services which it provides to the hinterland. Finally, limitations were placed upon the importance of the secondary centers:

A secondary center may be identified as an area of growth potential, but its proximity to the primary center and its position in that center's hinterland hinders its future growth and therefore the range and magnitude of public investments to be made in it. The public investment program for a secondary center must be related to the program for the growth area as a whole.

In setting its policies, the commission was attempting to give operational significance to some of the theoretical considerations discussed in the preceding chapter. Its emphasis was upon functions and linkages, not upon exports alone, for example. A reflection of the concept of a systematic relationship among urban places can be discerned. Even at this early point, the concept of the center as the source of public service delivery is also evident. In the evolution of policy, this theme took on increasingly greater significance.

Four aspects of these early actions proved to be highly important as time passed. First, particularly in the central part of the region, individual communities and their environs tended to be too small to economically justify public facilities in each of them. However, two or more neighboring centers might be able to provide complementary public services, if they were linked more closely through transportation improvements. An operating concept of treating communities that were separated by distance, but by minimal time, as an entity evolved. Doing so might enable them to achieve the economies associated with size that were a hallmark of a center. Commission policy encouraged this by explicitly defining a center as potentially consisting of more than one community.

Secondly, the commission action emphasized both the flow of people and resources to the center from the hinterland and also the flow of services to the residents of the hinterland. This emphasis on the mutual relationship of center and hinterland was designed to avoid developing a program that would benefit rural residents only if they moved to urban areas or as a result of economic activity spilling out into the surrounding area.

Third, and closely related to the second, is the emphasis on "other localities from which the population must be served." The commission policy avoided the rigidity of permitting investments only in "growth centers." It recognized that in some areas populations exist which cannot have access to certain services if they are provided only at these centers. In addition, some investments that serve a growth center need not or cannot be efficiently located in it.

Fourth, this emphasis on functionally efficient service delivery has had an impact on the commission's early distinction between primary and secondary centers. The original statement did not sufficiently circumscribe the commission's investments in metropolitan areas. It has now come to recognize a three-tiered hierarchy. Consideration is given to the function the center plays in its area and this has become the basis for distinguishing among the types of public expenditures deemed appropriate in each. Regional centers are in areas with the largest population density and the most extensive geographic hinterlands. They are thought to be the appropriate location of specialized facilities designed to serve a large area. In the middle range are primary centers, those in areas of some economic potential, which became the focus of both human resource serving investments and ones designed for direct economic stimulation. At the other extreme are secondary centers, those in areas of modest growth potential, which serve as service centers for typically dispersed populations. In these areas health and education investments are centered that can serve to upgrade the potentials of the people of the region and make them better able to compete for opportunities wherever they may choose to live.

The guidelines established are very general and do not define exact criteria by which growth areas are delineated. These are to be established by the individual states, a policy established for two reasons. First, the commission sought to establish a joint federal-state partnership which would capitalize on state participation in the development of individual strategies within an overall regional strategy. The approach was intended to allow for individual differences among the states while at the same time maintaining a unified point of view.

Second, there was a problem arising from the diversity of the Appalachian economy. Had the commission adopted more rigid guidelines, the result would have been a clustering of growth areas in the relatively more prosperous states and a paucity of growth areas in the less prosperous states. The Commission chose instead to establish a general policy. It provided technical advice to the states and encouraged them to establish their own criteria for defining growth areas, within that policy.

Though the commission policy toward growth area delineation was general and permissive, greater specificity was required in establishing guidelines for individual programs. In general, operating guidelines were devised with two goals in mind: to provide the basic facilities essential to the region's growth and to help to develop its human resources. These two goals are largely complementary because the development of human resources can directly improve prospects for economic performance. However, a competitive element is also present. The human resource development needs of the region's dispersed population sometimes requires investments be made at locations which are not likely to experience significant economic growth. In its resolutions establishing program and project evaluation criteria, the commission has sought investments that can serve both goals but has always created exceptions to allow for investments for human resource development when both goals could not be achieved. In addition, some programs have objectives that require investments outside growth areas.

The guidelines initially established for each program came from commission resolutions. Some have been modified on the basis of experience and later commission action but the basic structure has remained. Detailed information about the guidelines is provided in the commission code[9] and operating experience is discussed in Chapter 7. The following paragraphs briefly describe the criteria established.[10]

Local access roads . . . "shall serve industrial and commercial sites and parks and service areas which offer a prospect of significant employment opportunities in an area of significant potential for future growth. . . ." The commission also authorized access roads in recreation areas which may or may not be growth areas and to facilitate the use of educational facilities, wherever located. It will also consider access roads serving residential developments in growth areas and timber areas as the act specifies.

Demonstration Health Program

Among the objectives of this program is demonstrating . . . "that it is possible to make available modern, comprehensive health care in a variety of regions in Appalachia. . . ." Strict adherence to a growth area policy would severely limit the range of demonstrations possible. Consequently, the designated demonstration health program areas need not conform to designated growth areas.

Land Stabilization, Conservation, and Erosion
Control Program

This program was intended to achieve a "concentration of activities in program and geographic areas where the greatest economic impact will be felt," while "according preference to needy farmers within such areas." Each area selected must "be located in or serve an area identified as having a significant potential for future growth" or there must be assurance that projects to be assisted "will complement other actual or planned investments in the area to be served or otherwise have a demonstrable impact on the solution of problems or the development of potentials of the area to be served."

Mine Area Restoration

. . . "projects shall be located in, or shall serve areas of significant potential for future growth. . ." However, projects will be considered "which are not designed to serve growth areas . . . where it is shown that such projects will provide opportunities for substantial employment derived from recreational development. . . ."

Housing Assistance

The code requires that projects be located in areas with growth potential.

Vocational Education

"Highest priority is given to those projects that are located" in growth areas "so that they can contribute to both educational improvement and economic development." If, however, it can be demonstrated "that the education needs of an isolated population cannot be adequately served by facilities in a growth area, the Commission will consider projects outside growth areas."

Sewage Treatment Facilities

Projects must be located in a growth area or upstream from a growth area and have a direct and demonstrable relationship to the economic development of the growth area.

Supplemental Funds

Funds may be used to supplement federal grant-in-aid programs for construction and original equipment including all programs authorized under the Appalachian Act. Supplemental grants to projects authorized under the Appalachian Act must conform to the criteria of the code relating to them. Specific criteria are established for other programs.

Projects related to land and water resource development, such as those under the Land and Water Conservation Fund Act, must be located in growth areas or in areas where it can be shown that the project will provide significant employment opportunities from recreational potential.

Health care projects located in growth areas will receive the highest priority since "health facilities and services can be valuable assets in attracting private investment into the Appalachian Region." However, supplemental grants for "the construction or equipment of nursing home facilities are permitted only if it is demonstrated that the nursing home is related to the economic development of an area either because it is a part of, or has a close association with an existing or planned regional demonstration health center . . . or because it will provide care for long-term patients of an existing hospital facility. . . ."

Education projects outside of growth areas may be funded if it can be shown that the needs of an isolated population cannot be served effectively by the facilities or services in a growth area.

Priority for airport safety improvements is given to "regional airports serving areas in more than one state" and then to airports that receive (or may soon receive) air carrier service.

In general, these guidelines reflect the commission's attempt to strike a balance between the region's economic development and human resource requirements while recognizing that there was no conceptual basis for certainty about the appropriate balance. The criteria provide for so many exceptions to permit meeting human resource development requirements that the likelihood of achieving concentrated investments in growth areas may seem small. The degree of concentration achieved is discussed in Chapter 8. At this point, however, it should be noted that missing from the guidelines described is a means for obtaining the states' judgments of areas worthy of investment concentration. Also missing was a means for obtaining groups of recommended projects that would conform to the policies of the commission and further the development of the areas affected. The State Investment Plan was designed to overcome these omissions. These plans are part of a structure of planning instituted under the Appalachian Act. All these varieties of plans and a more specific understanding of the nature of regional planning are the subject of the following chapter.

6 Planning for Appalachian Development

Note was made earlier of the two forms of dissatisfaction that led to the adoption of the ARDA. Basic was the depressed scale of living that the name "Appalachia" came to connote. In an institutional, instrumental sense, equally dissatisfying was the performance of government as a servant of popular demands. The Appalachian Act sought improvements in this latter realm through the establishment of the Appalachian Regional Commission, the local development districts, and the concept of state responsibility for establishing area, program and project priorities. Hinted at, mentioned, but not fully enunciated, was the anticipation of a logical sequence of actions based on careful examination of conditions and consideration of alternatives. In a word, a plan was to be created, though no one could exactly define the nature of that plan, its coverage or its consequences. The evolution of regional planning, its authors, contents, and effects are the subject of this chapter.

The nature of Appalachian planning could be defined in 1965 in a negative sense. There were various planning models in operation that were inappropriate, so in this sense, a definition existed. But to know what it was not to be, was not a full guide to what it was to be.

First of all, in no sense was Appalachian regional planning to closely resemble planning of the Eastern or Western European style. The Eastern variety eschews the capitalist assumptions of the Appalachian effort. The Western depends on degrees of controls (for example, on industrial location) and the existence of some organized concept of national priorities (that might or might not be called a plan) that were absent from the American scene.

At the other extreme, it was understood that the ARA type of planning was not intended either. This had proved to be too parochial and static to be operationally useful.

Planning of the TVA variety was also not desired. This type has proceeded from a natural resource base and had tended to keep state government peripherally involved. Appalachian planning was to begin from a broader base and to have state governments centrally involved.

Appalachian planning was not to be city planning writ large. In relative terms, city planning is microscopic in its concern for land use, traffic circulation, public service siting and availability, and so forth. No regional agency could hope to acquire either the expertise or the concurrence that could lead to an acceptable plan of the city type for a region of roughly the size and population of California, with thousands of units of government whose powers are determined by numerous state constitutions and legislative acts.

The absence of a national development plan, or even enunciated strategy, added another specification of what Appalachian planning was not to be. It was not to be a sub-set of national objectives, stepped down in magnitude to the region's relative size.

The commission was largely free to plan as it chose, limited in program by the functional sections of its legislation and limited in conception by its financial and staff resources and by its view of the practical or realistically realizable programs that planning might recommend.

An understanding of its decisions on how to plan, what to plan, and what effects to anticipate requires an examination of the relationship between the planner and the politician. It also requires an understanding of the nature of the products planning produces.

The Politician, the Planner, and the Plan

There exists in the minds of some a belief that the planning process can proceed aloof from political influence until ready to present to the decision-maker a number of well-articulated alternatives, leaving the rendering of judgment to the politician at that point. This is an unrealistic view of the process. Planning and decision-making must communicate with each other throughout the process and not solely when "the alternatives" are available. During the process of planning, the planner must be aware of political realities just as he seeks to inform himself of physical, economic, social and cultural realities. He would not think he was doing a craftsman-like job if he omitted consideration of any of the last four of these, and it is equally true that his work would be deficient if he omitted consideration of the first. Just as certain approaches or alternatives may be technically unfeasible or impractical, the same can be true of their political feasibility and practicality. And somewhat analogous to the movement of a mountain or a river, the planning program, when wisely done, can help alter political feasibility.

Attempts to isolate planning from politics stem from the politician's fear that the planner will usurp his prerogatives and from the planner's fear that the politician will besmirch the technical integrity of his work. In an atmosphere such as this, in which two principal actors are jealous of and distrust each other, it is difficult to see how a standard of cooperation can be established as an example for all whose assistance will be required to effectuate a plan. Ideological acceptance of division of labor and consequent dependence upon one another is the first and most basic requirement for the marriage of planning and the political process. The nature of the marriage is not simple to specify and, as with all such arrangements, it must reflect the personalities of the partners. Respect for each other and each other's contribution would seem to be crucial.

Out of this relationship can come the most useful, though invisible, product of planning and the research which is basic to it. The impact of planning stems not only from the production of a "product" (a report or document) but from continuous translation and application of that product in the program itself. The interaction of the planner and the politician can provide mutual guidance that can subtly, and sometimes dramatically, alter directions.

Perhaps the greatest impact of planning comes from the myriad of subtle influences it can exert on thinking. The public payoff and prestige are undoubtedly greatest when profound new insights are revealed and new, hopeful directions illuminated. Such contributions are rare. On balance, the unheralded contributions probably have greater significance. The real products of planning may well be the gradual shifts in program emphasis, the changes in understanding of dynamic processes, the alterations in implicit dimensions of objectives whose literal wording remains unchanged.

Impacts of this variety are beyond the range of any except testimonial commentary. Despite this, they are no less real than those that can be explicitly identified, to be discussed shortly.

Implicit Impacts of Planning

During the years of the commission's operations, there has been a shift and elaboration of understanding of the growth oriented approach which underlies the entire program. The early understanding was concerned with the economic function of growth centers. They were viewed as places that attracted resources and provided economies for industrial operation which made them the centers from which income (and later employment) flowed into the surrounding hinterlands. As examination of, and operation in, the region progressed, a subtle shift of thinking took place. Borrowing from central place theory and its hierarchy of urban places, there evolved a concept of a hierarchy of public service delivery centers that was superimposed upon the growth center concept. A growth center came to be viewed as potentially discharging two functions, the economic function initially contemplated plus a public service delivery function for its area by providing it with health and education services, for example. Though never stated explicitly, the basic policy prescription of the act came to be reinterpreted. The words "concentrated in areas where there is a significant potential for future growth, and where the expected return on the public dollars invested will be the greatest" remained the same. Increased emphasis came to be placed on the latter part of the clause. The "return on the public dollars invested" was increasingly evaluated in public service delivery terms, as well as income and job creation terms.

A number of factors account for this. First, some state portions of the region had only the meagerest opportunities to qualify for investments under the first part of the clause. Secondly, from the beginning, the commission recognized an obligation and opportunity to serve the people of the region with public services. Means to accomplish this were continuously sought. Thirdly, growth potential in a strictly economic sense is an imprecise concept and investments appropriate to serve it, an even more imprecise one. Lastly, there were sound efficiency reasons to adopt this interpretation.

Many Appalachian communities have resident populations that are too small to operate efficiently scaled public service facilities. Up to a certain size, decreases in cost per unit occur as facility size increases, particularly in education and health. These unit cost decreases are only attainable if the service area is expanded to include the surrounding population. This is true throughout much of the nation but particularly true of Appalachia, with its very dense but non-urban population distribution. The only efficient way to provide services in the centers, which would also make them attractive to private investment and job creation, was to consider them as service delivery centers to surrounding areas as well. As a result, there evolved an informal hierarchical structure of service delivery centers, some providing high-cost, specialized health and education services to a large territory and population, others serving a lesser area with more general services, and still others providing rather elementary services to an even smaller service area. Explicit hierarchical structures of this kind were developed in some states for both health and education but, of equal importance, there was implicit acceptance of the concept of such a structure. This acceptance among all the states has affected the scale and scope of individual projects in unmeasurable and even unconscious ways. Acceptance of the concept and its application is neither uniform nor enforced but the shift to a broadened interpretation of the policy prescription of the act is very real.

Another important shift has been the change in understanding the process of economic development in Appalachia. The PARC report had pointed to the lack of urbanization in the region and to the evolution of the national economy into one emphasizing non-manufacturing, or service, employment. However, the full implications of these facts were only gradually grasped and articulated into the program. Essentially, the change has been to an emphasis on service employment as a principal opportunity. It was seen as the hallmark of the last stage of development, as emphasized in the stages theory of development. Though not forgotten by any means, extraction and manufacturing were less frequently thought to be likely future mainstays of the regional economy. The type of thinking associated with export base theory became less dominant.

The change in emphasis occurred in a sequence that began with acceptance of the principle that the region was a part of the national economy and that it would have to work with national trends to find a fulfilling role in it. It would therefore have to offer competitive locations and public services to the most rapidly growing segments of the national economy, the service industries. Note was then taken that with exceptions such as some parts of the recreation industry, service industries are necessarily urban in character since most of them must move to markets rather than moving their products to market. This led to the conclusion that a serious handicap in the development of the Appalachian economy was the paucity of urban places in parts of the region and the degraded quality of many that existed throughout the region. This disposed the commission to an intense concern with the pattern of national urban growth and the debates over national urban policy. It also led to the conclusion that the regional strategy must contain, as a major component, the selective strengthening of existing, or potential new, urban centers, those judged to be the ones most likely to grow in service employment on the basis of their location and performance and potential.

These two gradual changes—the increased emphasis on the public service delivery functions of centers and on private service industries as significant providers of employment—were complementary and had two significant effects.

First, they helped substantially in the development guidelines for the appropriate location and size of public facilities. They added a rationale and some specificity to the implementation of the mandate that "the public dollars invested" be expended with economic efficiency.

Secondly, they combined with the existing commitment to enhance the quality of Appalachian's lives. As it became increasingly evident that the quality of urban life and the public services available in Appalachia's cities and towns would significantly affect the Region's ability to reach its economic goals, a rationale for greater emphasis on human resource investments emerged.

In common with most agencies, the commission expresses its priorities by the relative size of its requests for funding of various sections of its act. These relative priorities have been reasonably well reflected in the funding levels provided, since Congress and the Bureau of the Budget (now Office of Management and Budget) have generally followed the Commission's relative rankings. Leaving out of consideration for the moment the funds for the highway program,[1] there has been a dramatic shift in relative emphasis. PARC recommended slightly more than 50 cents for human resource programs for each dollar of non-highway physical resource programs. For the first biennium of operation the ratio of the two was close to 1:1. By the end of fiscal 1971, the ratio of appropriations was three to one in favor of human resources. No single paper or set of papers will document the role that planning played in initiating and propelling the changes in understanding that lie behind these changes in program emphasis but they are a result of it.

Regional Planning

The identifiable, explicit planning products and processes that developed under the commission aegis divide logically into four categories—those of regional scope, those embracing major sub-regions, plans for each state, and plans for sub-state units. This division is itself indicative of the basic planning decision that was reached. In most respects, Appalachia is too diverse politically, economically, socially, and in resources to be treated as a planning entity. With the exceptions of the regional plans to be discussed, regional planning in the Appalachian context is to be understood as the development of general regional goals, regional strategies, and regional policy instruments but with state or area specific goals, priorities and institutional adaptations to accomplish them. Thus there cannot exist a regional plan in the sense of a single comprehensive document that defines goals, programs, projects and other activities for each individual area.

Explicit planning products for the region clearly pre-date the Appalachian Regional Commission. In a sense, the plan for the National Pike into the West from Cumberland, Maryland was the first Appalachian highway plan. Certainly, the PARC report has to be viewed as a basic planning document which largely determined the approach the current effort would take and the tools available to it. The present commission, therefore, decided that its planning for the region as a whole had to be at a much more specific level. It had been granted a set of tools by the Congress and it needed to know how and where to apply them. It also needed to know how the tools might need to be reshaped and what additions to the available list might be sought because they could be effectively utilized. Regionwide planning has therefore tended to be related to functional program planning. Some, such as the functional plans for highways and education and health and natural resources (other than water) are so intimately connected with the program's operations that discussion of them is reserved for Chapter 8 where the various functional areas are discussed. At this point, only three region-wide functional area planning studies will be examined, those relating to timber development, airports, and water resources.

Timber Development

In the transition from the 1964 version of the Appalachian Act to the one passed in 1965, the language of Section 204 relating to timber development organizations underwent substantial revision. The original version permitted the creation of timber development corporations that were empowered to consolidate small landholdings and to integrate their operations, going from timber harvesting through the production of products made of wood to the marketing of such products. These were to be profit-making entities which could receive initial capital from a bond-issuing regional development corporation. The regional corporation idea succumbed to charges of "backdoor financing" (i.e., access to public credit without direct appropriational accountability) and the timber corporation idea suffered a similar fate for a complex of reasons, not the smallest of which was the opposition of dominant buyers in a market whose sellers are small and fragmented. What passed congressional muster was a program of loans and technical assistance to non-profit timber development organizations. The loans were not to be available for the marketing, processing or manufacturing of forest products and could only be used for land consolidation on a demonstration basis. In addition, research into uses for the region's hardwood resources were authorized.

The act as passed meant that a timber development organization would probably have to be an association or cooperative whose members joined their typically separated holdings under a timber management agreement. They would experience financial benefits as their individual holdings produced a better crop due to the scientific management that would be available to them at a lower cost than they could obtain it individually. The basic question was whether private landholders, given their many reasons for holding timber tracts, would find it advantageous to participate in such an undertaking and what alternative forms such an organization might adopt. To help answer this, a study[2] was commissioned that concluded that given the restrictions in the law, it was unlikely that interest in such organizations would warrant their initiation.

The commission then decided to support use of some of the funds appropriated for Section 204 by the Department of Agriculture which is providing advice to groups in New York, Kentucky, North Carolina and Tennessee who are devising alternative structures for timber development organizations. No funds beyond the initial appropriation of $600,000 have been made available under this section.

It can properly be asked why the commission adopted such a passive role in implementing this section of the act when, in other cases, it sought altered and widened authority. Two factors seem to be explanatory. First, many of the apparently reasonable alternatives had been rejected by the Congress already. Secondly, no one could visualize a sufficiently beneficial effect on a large enough area or for large enough numbers of people to warrant using some of the region's credit of goodwill in the Congress in an attempt to perfect this section of the act.

In summary, in this case the application of planning led to virtually no program but this does provide a good example of the interaction of the economic, social and political realities that condition a planning program. The results of the early study plus the political environment meant that timber development would not consume any substantial commission planning resources.

Airports

No section of the Appalachian Act is specifically concerned with airport investments but funds provided under Section 214 can be used to supplement grant funds available for this purpose through the Federal Aviation Administration. Uncertainty about the most appropriate use of 214 funds for this purpose led to the development of a regional airport plan.[3] In general, what the commission sought was a means of projecting the economic development effects of airport availability, the likely demand for air travel, the geographic location of airports with air carrier service that would maximize air service availability, an indication of the appropriate role of general aviation airports in the region, a description of the improvements likely to be required at existing and new airports, and an estimate of the funding level required. Issues of this nature arose for several reasons—some states were indicating an intention to encourage numerous airports as an industrial attraction device; some states were concerned that the development of more airports would so fragment the air carrier market that no facility could supply sufficient passengers to preserve the current availability of service; some sought guidance on questions of facility consolidation, location of new facilities, and upgrading of facilities to permit their use by jet aircraft.

The final product received by the commission addressed all these issues, but despite this, its impact on the program is both difficult to assess and less than might be hoped. This is true because the commission can only supplement grants approved by the FAA. As a result, implementation depended upon FAA approval of the suggested projects. This would have required that FAA accept economic development effects as a factor in assigning priorities to projects as the ARC plan recommended, in addition to their normal criterion of air commerce needs. FAA did distribute the airport plan to its regional offices, where it was given consideration when their contributions to the National Airport Plan were developed. However, the FAA was not willing to accept economic development impact as a criterion for its own grants. Thus the effect of the plan on the airport program was limited to its use by the states and the commission in deciding which FAA grants in the region to supplement and whether to accord airport investments a high priority in allocating 214 funds.

Less than 3.5% of the 214 funds available have been used to supplement airport grants, largely at locations specified in the plan. Only judgment can decide whether this figure might have been higher if no airport plan had been prepared. It seems reasonable that this might have been the case.[4]

The plan provided support for state administrators in making the potentially sensitive decision to turn down applicants. They also knew that gross departures from the regional plan would lead to questioning by the ARC staff and possibly to a request for reconsideration of the project proposal by the state.

The commission's airport plan experience seems to confirm the hoary wisdom that planning without control over the funds needed to implement the plan is likely to be futile and that the degree of futility diminishes as the degree of control over funds increases. This is true for individual functional programs and it is also true for the overall program, as is evident in the case of the regional commissions established under Title V of the Public Works and Economic Development Act of 1965.[5]

Water Resources

The Water Resource Survey authorized under Sec. 206 is the prime example of planning done for the region but not under the direct leadership of the commission. The Secretary of the Army (through the Army Corps of Engineers) was directed to "prepare a comprehensive plan for the development and efficient utilization of the water and related resources of the Appalachian region . . . integral and harmonious (with) the regional economic development program . . . coordinated with all comprehensive river basin plans heretofore or hereafter developed." For this purpose, $5 million was authorized and appropriated. The report, after comment by the commission, was to have been submitted to Congress by Dec. 31, 1968. At this writing, it has not been officially transmitted to the commission.

The tardiness of the report is only one reflection of the magnitude of the technical and political task Sec. 206 required. From the technical standpoint, harmony with the regional development program required both an articulated regional program early in the commission's existence and a means of incorporating the effects of water resources development into that program. Even if the regional program had been immediately available (which it was not), the conventional means of assessing the impact of water resource development were not designed to accommodate concepts like "enhancing potential for growth" or "inducing growth." The Water Resource Survey therefore had to expand the criteria on which projects are evaluated from the traditional comparison of narrowly defined costs and benefits. It had to try to estimate, on the benefit side, the incomes generated by activities induced into being. On the cost side, estimates of the costs of all required investments (public and private) had to be made. Significant analytical problems were encountered in devising tools to measure these concepts and, though progress was made, the difficult issues are far from fully resolved.

From the political standpoint, two types of difficulties were encountered. First, the survey was ordered to be conducted in consultation with the commission, the federal Departments of Agriculture, Commerce, Health, Education and Welfare, and Interior, the Tennessee Valley Authority and the Federal Power Commission. In keeping with the joint nature of the commission, each of the Appalachian states was added to this list. Each of these organizations (with the exception of the Commission) had an on-going program or programs which it advocated as a potent contributant to regional improvement, if only it could be enlarged or expanded. Since no fiscal limit had been imposed on the program to be recommended, it was difficult to force priorities on the participants. Though extensive pruning of recommendations occurred, the report as finally submitted by the Corps to the Secretary of the Army included many hundreds of projects at an unknown probable future cost, that could probably reach many billions over the next 20 to 30 years.

The technical problem of benefit and cost evaluation, plus this first political problem of setting program priorities, combined to form a second type of political problem. Clearly, the technical criteria established were not capable of reducing the list of desired projects to fiscally manageable proportions. Rather, under the rubric of regional economic development, a key appeared to have been found that potentially opened the federal treasury to many projects that would not have been eligible for funding before. Both the commission and the Office of Management and Budget, as well as the Secretary of the Army, had to wrestle hard to keep the potential benefit to the region from a broader look at the effects of water resource projects from being submerged in an excess of water resource costs. That struggle continues.

The technical issues raised by the Water Resources Survey are of national significance and means of resolving them have been elaborated by the Water Resources Council as a new procedure for evaluating all water resource projects. Essentially, the question raised is how many of the impacts of water resource development do we choose to highlight and make available for explicit evaluation in determining public expenditures. The answer might appear obvious but in the absence of acceptable techniques for making this display, it is possible to have even more confusion and less precision than the present imprecise system provides. The Appalachian water report has been delayed while these national issues have been examined further. In the meantime, some individual projects listed in the report to the secretary have proceeded, though without any additional impetus that issuance of the report might provide.

If there are generalizable lessons for regional planning that can be distilled from this, they are first, that innovations are hard to develop and even harder to get accepted and secondly, that a fiscal target is an essential planning tool. Had one been in existence, the number of projects in the Appalachian water survey would have been diminished and its acceptability enhanced. It may be argued that you cannot have a fiscal target without a plan, just as it is here argued that effective planning requires a sense of fiscal reality. If anything, this reasserts the need for harmonious communication between the planner and the politician. It also provides a rationale for the use by the commission of allocation formulas to divide appropriated funds among the states, as described in the next chapter.

Sub-Regional Plans

Repeatedly, mention has been made of the disparate nature of the Appalachian region. It is not homogeneous in topography, potentials or problems and the commission has recognized this fact in numerous ways, for example in the practice of encouraging state plans and state priorities which is the subject of later pages of this chapter. At the supra-state level, numerous commission statements speak of the four Appalachias, a division of the region into four generalized areas whose boundaries are not precise but which generally follow the boundaries on the following map.

In its 1970 *Annual Report,*[6] the commission described these areas as follows:

Southern Appalachia

"The first of these major sub-regions is Southern Appalachia, covering Mississippi, Alabama, South Carolina, and parts of Georgia, Tennessee, North Carolina,

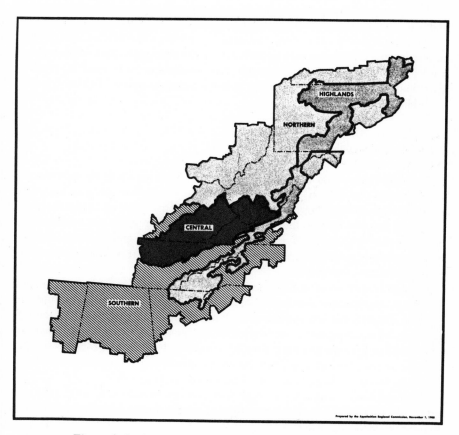

Figure 6-1. Appalachian Region: The Four Appalachias.

and Virginia. Industrialization and urbanization are occurring here quite rapidly, converting the area from an agricultural economy to manufacturing and services. New production jobs are being generated in such fields as apparel, textiles, and food processing. While much of this growth has been initially low-wage and female-employing, several areas have already begun to diversify beyond these labor intensive industries.

"The first priority in Southern Appalachia is the development of an educational system capable of providing a labor force competitive with that of the nation as a whole. While many states are attempting to strengthen primary and secondary education on their own, all the states have recognized the need under the Appalachian Program to provide high school and post-high school level vocational and technical education on a large scale for the apparent growth industries in the South. New industries now developing in Southern Appalachia also require professional personnel, and the states are concentrating on the development of higher educational opportunities relevant to those growth opportunities.

"Second priority has been assigned to public facilities in the growing industrial communities where growth has come so rapidly that it threatens to choke itself off before the people can realize its full benefits. In such communities, Appalachian assistance is being used to develop a full complement of public facilities.

Northern Appalachia

"The second sub-region is Northern Appalachia, encompassing the southern tier of New York and most of the Allegheny Plateau area in Pennsylvania, Maryland, northern West Virginia, and southern Ohio. This part of Appalachia has problems related to the transition from dependence on a coal-steel-railroad economy to new types of manufacturing and service employment. Primary emphasis has been placed upon post-high school and adult occupational training to facilitate this transition.

"Many communities suffer from environmental problems, legacies of past industrial and mining activities, including mine drainage pollution, mine subsidence, blight from strip mining, and mine fires and flooding. Community renewal and environmental improvements are the most pressing needs for future growth. High priority has been given to solving environmental problems through the use of mine area restoration, water pollution control, housing assistance, supplemental grant funds, and other Federal and state programs.

"In addition, a number of local governments in the area, with assistance under the Appalachian Act, are investigating organizational and financial reforms to improve their effectiveness.

Appalachian Highlands

"The third sub-region is the Appalachian Highlands, which begins near Mt. Oglethorpe in Georgia and extends through the Great Smoky, Blue Ridge, Allegheny and Catskill Mountains. Covering parts of Georgia, South Carolina, Tennessee, New York, North Carolina, Kentucky, Virginia, West Virginia, Pennsylvania, and Maryland, the Highlands is a sparsely populated segment of Appalachia rich in scenic beauty and recreation potential and close to the heavily-populated metropolitan areas of the East, Midwest, and South.

Central Appalachia

"The last of the four major sub-regions is Central Appalachia, covering 60 counties in eastern Kentucky, southern West Virginia, southwestern Virginia, and northern Tennessee, where urbanization must be accelerated if adequate services and employment opportunities are to be developed for their million and half people. Only 250,000 persons live in communities of more than 2,500. The choice is between faster growth of key communities or continued outmigration. Four initial priorities have been established: transportation, education, health, and concerted development of key communities in the area."

In cooperation with the states affected, the commission undertook the creation of development plans for two of these sub-regions, Central Appalachia and the Highlands. In each case, the ultimate objective was similar, to discern the dimensions of the problems and opportunities that could be the basis for collaborative programs. Undertakings of this nature can have two different levels of goals, however. One set might be the development of a phased plan of implementation with discrete, complementary tasks assigned to the various agencies with operating responsibilities. The other would be for the collaborators to agree on an understanding of the nature of the problems and potentials. This understanding then becomes fundamentally influential in shaping the largely independent programs and practices they initiate or conduct. Discretion remains in each organization's hands that allows it to adjust to fiscal and other influences as they appear. However, agreement exists and persists about the general route to be taken and the destination to be reached. Goals of this type are less intellectually satisfying since at the completion of the planning process, no set of "marching orders" exists. They can, however be far more pragmatically useful. They preserve the values, independence and flexibility of the agencies involved, avoid the probably sterile—and sterilizing—debates over prerogatives and responsibilities, and depend upon intellectual commitment rather than legal or power constraints to achieve the goals sought.

It may be argued that this latter set of goals is likely to be inefficient, that it can lead to duplicating, even competitive actions, that sequencing can be wrong and that commitments fade if not enforced. This is all true. It is also true that in an altered way, this is an adaptation of an unbalanced growth approach, since it economizes on scarce managerial talent. The more formal approach clearly requires a far higher commitment of authority and supervision. It also requires an ability to know and foresee the consequences of a series of acts that may far exceed our present capabilities. This results in uncertainty that makes reconciling disagreements during plan preparation exceedingly difficult since no one can demonstrate causes and their effects unambiguously. For this reason, agreement on a fixed sequence of events by independent bodies tends to be rare and may probably be undesirable. Flexibility and adaptation are more to be desired than the inflexibility of a rigid plan born of compromise since an alteration of the plan re-opens all the old compromises.

Central Appalachia

The plan for Central Appalachia[7] prepared by the commission, with assistance from the states and several federal agencies (including partial funding by HUD under its 701 planning grant program), is of the less rigid variety. At the outset, no one sought or desired a formal plan that would stipulate action and date and agency responsible. Far more useful, it was thought, would be a careful look at the depressed 60 counties in Kentucky, Tennessee, Virginia and West Virginia that were in the heart of Appalachia and the basic occasion for the program. The product was to be an accepted strategy based on an understanding of what were the reasonably possible sets of actions to upgrade the lives and widen the opportunities of the 1.5 million residents.

Numerous dimensions were examined—income, employment, population characteristics, education, health, banking, manufacturing, transportation, topography, population density, dispersion and urbanization, governments, and more. The basic product from the process was an agreement on a strategy that appeared to accommodate the historical facts and trends, the aspirations of the citizens, and the programs available or likely to become available.

It was this study, more than any other single event, that crystallized the transformation of the growth center strategy from a largely economic approach to one that also included public service delivery. The study made clear that for many years to come, the area would continue to be densely populated, that many small communities in the area were so constrained by their topography and location that they were unlikely to grow in numbers though they served a numerous hinterland population, that the area's decline in employment was ending, that manufacturing and (in selected locations) service employment would grow, that improving transportation was concurrent with manufacturing growth, that education, individual health, and environmental health problems were virtually universal, that the condition of housing and public service facilities were generally deplorable, and that there were too many weak units of government.

The strategy which crystallized was one of physically concentrated investments, located to reach hinterland populations, with emphasis on outreach facilities and new techniques for delivering public service. The importance of the area's modest urban places was emphasized and, where reasonably proximate, consideration of two or more of them as a single entity, sharing facilities and the delivery of services was also needed. Intergovernmental cooperation received additional emphasis, as did investment in the people of the area. Though a continuing population was expected, continued out-migration would occur and whether ultimately residents of Central Appalachia or not, the present citizens were presently deprived in many relevant dimensions.

The Central Appalachian study recommended no specific sequence of acts so no one can gauge later performance against a specification of intentions. The results were more amorphous. They were, if anything, subtle changes in attitudes, more realistic assessments of opportunities, more compatible sets of anticipations among many agencies and individuals. Their presence cannot be measured and their impact is certainly unknowable. What can be said is that the structure of institutional behavior since has tended to follow the strategy that evolved. Whether it would have anyway, no one can say.

Highlands

Predating the PARC report, with its comments on the recreation potential of the Appalachian Highlands, prescriptions and recommendations for the area had commonly spoken of this opportunity. Though generally deficient in lakes and man-made impoundments, the area is among the most rugged in the Eastern United States, is heavily forested and very large acreages are in the public domain, either federal or state. Communities in the area which recognized their likely inability to develop a strong manufacturing sector supported their aspirations for development with reference to their scenic and locational advantages and the enlarging share of discretionary expenditures on recreation in the national income.

If anything, the enthusiasm for recreation as an industry seemed to be overly developed at the time the commission began its operations. No one had carefully thought about a series of relevant questions, the first of which was, is recreation a desirable base for an area economy and the second, are there any conditions that increase the likelihood of its having desirable effects. Even preliminary answers to these questions would enable the states and the commission to allocate expenditures among the many competing demands and apparent opportunities.

The initial research undertaken,[8] therefore, was designed to assess the degree of favorable impact on the host areas that recognizably successful recreation destination areas had had (whether in or out of Appalachia), and to develop criteria for judging what local conditions apparently needed to be present for favorable effects to appear. In summary, the conclusions were that recreation tends to be a low paying and intermittent employer, that its peak labor demands frequently cause labor importation (and almost immediately, the export of a share of the incomes generated), that expenditures of recreationists are an increasing function of the duration of their stay (among other factors), and that the degree of favorable impact on the local economy depended upon its ability to provide services complementary to the recreation industry (for example, laundry and food wholesaling services). Ironically, the local benefits from recreation were the larger (everything else remaining the same), the closer the recreation area was to a large urban place.

These conclusions added a note of caution and realistic concern to the prior tendency to prescribe becoming "Switzerland" to every area that was unlikely to become the "Rhur." Three other factors tended to temper enthusiasm and retard the pace of Commission-sponsored investments. The first of these was a growing recognition that despite Appalachia's position astride a logical recreation destination area for the East Coast and Midwest, the market was not limitless. The development of an excessive number of destination areas, added to the ones in existence, could fragment the market to such an extent that, especially in the early years, financial success for all might be jeopardized. Secondly, the use of the land for recreation, which has such a large scenic component, would require attention to possible competing uses, such as mining or timbering, and to possible complementary uses, such as impoundments, either publicly or privately sponsored. A third important factor was the fact that so much of the land involved was in public ownership. In some ways, this made planning for the Highlands easier but, in other ways, the issue was complicated as a result. Ease arose, obviously, because agreement among agencies did not have to be followed by land acquisition or zoning or other controls on private land holders. Complications arose because of the differing legislative mandates of the agencies, their differing interpretations of their mandates, and the differing segments of the public they considered to be their prime constituents. However, it was possible to conceive of a planning process that could go beyond the objectives of the Central Appalachian plan. It was conceivable that somewhat more precise commitments to action could be developed as a result of the Highlands planning effort, though the problems of dealing with a multiplicity of agencies and reconciling their differences remained.

The planning effort was approached in a series of steps, during each of which the affected state and federal agencies were a party to the design, implementation, and review. Initially, a judgmental screening of existing and potential recreation areas produced a list of 23 recreation destination areas of possible future significance. From this list, 14 of the best prospects were picked for further study. Estimates of the recreation demand likely to be generated in the future in the region and in the areas surrounding it were made and appropriate shares allocated to these 14 areas, as well as to other uses of recreation time.[9] These estimates of demand implied the existence of suitably attractive facilities at these locations, so the succeeding step involved the preparation of site development plans for each area, to be followed by a more detailed implementation plan, including the actions needed to be taken by public and private bodies to achieve the degree of use estimated. These actions become the responsibility of the implementing agencies, who presumably have indicated that they are persuaded of their desirability because of their concurrence in the earlier step of the process and the conclusions that resulted.

At the time of this writing, the last steps in the planning procedure are just being taken. It is too soon to know the extent to which implementation will follow conception. Ideally, a sound plan has been developed and implementation will occur. But even if the plan is ideal, it is too much to expect precise implementation. Public agencies have changes in leadership, legislative mandates and constituency pressures. At best, they can create the pre-conditions for private investment, in the many cases where this is anticipated, but cannot assure its timely and appropriately scaled appearance. As a result, even a sub-regional plan that comes closer to assigning "marching orders" cannot and need not be highly specific. Great specificity masks uncertainty and may engender anticipations of strict adherence in implementation that are likely to be frustrated. A judgmentally defined degree of specificity that gives sufficient assurance to all other potential actors (public and private) so that they are encouraged to carry out their roles, combined with sufficient flexibility to adjust to changing opportunities and obstacles, is probably the most useful attribute of a plan for the Highlands.

State Planning

An innovative feature of the Appalachian endeavor is the participation of the states in decisions on the allocation and expenditure of federal funds. The state plan can be viewed as a means of regularizing the exercise of this function. The joint federal-state nature of the commission makes emphasis on judgments and analyses at this level appropriate. Even more, the supposition in law and policy is that the vantage point and responsibility of the state uniquely qualify it to make crucial operational decisions. In concept, however, the state plan was intended to be even more than this. Hopefully, it was to initiate a more planful approach to the general exercise of state governmental powers and to increase the authority of the governors who, in many states, are legally and institutionally inhibited in the exercise of the function of chief executive.

The following chapter will concern itself largely with the legal and institutional situation in which the commission has operated, and offers comments on the effectiveness of state planning. Here, emphasis will be on the content of the state plan itself and its evaluation in the hands of the commission.[10] It is essential to recognize at this point, however, some of the political context in which this planning experience has occurred.

At the time that the program was initiated, it was frequently contended by critics of its concept of federal-state partnership that the states would not be able to discharge the technically and politically difficult obligation of announcing areas of geographic and program emphasis in which funds would be concentrated. It was argued that the planning that had occurred in those states with any experience at all in the field had been largely or totally remote from and irrelevant for actual state activities. There was no competence bred of experience in most states on which to build. Moreover, the political hazards for the governors were deemed to be so great that judgments of the type expected were unlikely to be made. The governor would have no state legislative constraints on which to rely in explaining to disappointed applicants why their requests could not be honored. The decisions about which projects to recommend were to be his alone and on the principle that elected officers find it difficult to frustrate constituents, the anticipation was that there would be a breakdown in a system that required the exercise of gubernatorial power.

In fact, these fears have not been realized. A number of explanations can be offered. First, apparently in some states the governors were seeking the leverage to exercise greater administrative controls and the program gave them the occasion for this. Secondly, the commission implicitly recognized the difficulties associated with plan preparation. It has been willing to adopt broad criteria and to accept documents that are less than ideal for the purposes for which they were designed. In fact, a basis for criticism of the commission exists because it has not progressively raised its standards even though the quality of state plans has generally been improving. The third, and perhaps most important reason for the frustration of these fears, has been the existence of the commission itself. Of course, its staff provided technical assistance in plan preparation but far more than that, its existence provided a convenient reason for the governor to use when deciding matters in ways he probably would have preferred anyway. For example, when pressed for an explanation about why certain projects were not recommended, the state could "pass the buck" by arguing that "they" (the commission) had established requirements that forbade worthwhile activities, such as those being proposed. As long as it was not stated that commission actions have virtually always been unanimous, an exterior force could be used to buttress the state's fortitude and judgment. The existence of the commission added both conscience and courage to state administration, at least insofar as Appalachian funds were concerned.

The requirements for State Investment Plans as stated in the commission code are, as suggested, general in nature. The state is expected to assess the problems and potentials of its entire Appalachian area, designate the centers whose potentials for growth are to be encouraged, develop long-term priorities among programs for improving the opportunities of its Appalachian population, and submit an annual "package" or list of projects which it believes are justified in light of the preceding analysis and priorities. The code speaks of annual updatings of the plan, though in fact, many times these have been slight alterations, as was probably appropriate. Neither analytical techniques, nor capacity to use them, nor problems and potentials change frequently. Annual project packages are submitted whose relevance to the plan are assessed. Once the plan and package have been approved, each individual project is then subject to technical review but not to questioning about its basic suitability.

The generality of these requirements, the lack of specificity about techniques to be employed, the lack of requirements for hinterland designations around centers, the lack of constraint on the number of centers in a state, the absence of any standards by which priorities for projects or their sequencing are to be set, all are evidence of the commission's intent that these be distinctive products of each state. There was awareness of lack of precision in the technical aspect of these decisions as well as awareness of the political nature of the fundamental decisions about objectives and program priorities.

The approval of a state plan and the projects identified in it is not a mechanical process of comparing the submission with an ideal set of criteria or with a separate analysis prepared by the commission staff. As indicated, the commission proceeded on the belief that no single best set of standards exists. Moreover, the commission and its staff are not separate from the states. In many cases the staff participated in the plan's development and were aware of the political and technical issues that were resolved in the document as submitted.

However, plan approval has not been automatic. Commission review involves perspectives broader than that of one state—the other states, the federal interest, and the region as a whole. This has led to numerous sets of conversations, sometimes relating to individual projects but also to the basic formulation of the plan, its geographic and functional area coverage, the anticipations and criteria implicit in it, and the effect of all of these on the nature and dispersion of investments.

In effect, the give-and-take of plan review has evolved a "common law" of standards that relate not solely to the technical process of plan development but also to the qualitative judgment of the suitability of the proposal, measured against the commission's evolving understanding of the problems and potentials of parts of the region and the effectiveness of various programs in given settings.

This set of evolved standards can be summarized by delineating six types of areas into which Appalachia can be divided and the types of programs appropriate to each.

a. *Areas within the range of influence of major metropolitan areas outside of Appalachia where regional development programs can capitalize on develop-*

ment opportunities pressing outward from those metropolitan areas. Examples of areas under such influence in Appalachia are the Hagerstown area of Maryland and the extreme eastern part of the Eastern Panhandle in West Virginia close to Washington and Baltimore; the area surrounding Atlanta; a small area in eastern Kentucky near Lexington; those portions of Appalachian Ohio near Cincinnati; portions of New York and Pennsylvania between Buffalo and Cleveland; and portions of eastern Pennsylvania and New York near New York and Philadelphia.

b. *Areas within the orbit of major Appalachian metropolitan centers* such as Pittsburgh, Birmingham, or Charleston, where dual programs must be undertaken to reinforce the service base and employment opportunities in the city while at the same time the surrounding rural area is more effectively integrated and linked to the area economy through improvements in transportation, health, education, and resource development.

c. *Areas unserved by any urban complex large enough to be capable of self-sustaining growth, but where there are many small towns close together,* the program should help develop complementary services so that together they offer the same service advantages and employment concentrations as a middle-sized city. The Pikeville-Prestonburg-Paintsville or Middlesboro-London-Corbin areas of eastern Kentucky or the Dalton-Calhoun area of Georgia are representative of this kind of area.

d. *Large Appalachian cities located in peculiar topographical situations* where a "critical mass" of population and social overhead exists, but where further growth within the city as presently defined is unlikely for lack of available land. Here initial efforts should concentrate on alternative ways for such cities to join with surrounding jurisdictions where growth will occur in order to preserve existing overhead in the city and make duplication of those services in the outlying areas unnecessary. Examples of such cities are Johnstown, Pennsylvania; Wheeling, West Virginia; and the central anthracite communities of northeastern Pennsylvania.

e. *Areas with a dense, but rural non-farm, population where there is no viable community and few urban services or urban centers.* A combination of two approaches may be required in these areas; one may be similar to the third strategy above; the other is a "new community" approach in which an urban center is consciously induced based on analysis that indicates that access, market, and demographic conditions are such that a viable urban center can be created.

f. *Areas that are sparsely populated but which have had conferred upon them unusual access and resource advantages which make it probable that development and migration of population will occur.* In such areas a planned "new community" approach may be indicated.

Plan preparation and plan review can be summarized as a five-step process of:

1. Delineation by the states of multicounty areas with common social, political, and economic interests.

2. The designation of the centers in each of these by the states.

3. The selection by the states from this list of centers of those that are to receive investment emphasis.

4. The recommendation by the states of the investments for these selected centers.

5. Review and refinement by the commission and the states of the plan presented.

Comments on the quality and usefulness of these plans are reserved for the next chapter but here it can be noted that as a result of this planning, new methodologies were created in some cases and in others, unique solutions were found. Errors have inevitably been made in this process, some of which have been corrected. Without doubt, a great deal of room for improvement remains. However, given the state of the art in this field, the process of improvement must be an evolutionary one of experimentation, during which individual states will develop solutions suited to their unique characteristics and needs.

No attempt has been made here to determine whether the places chosen for program concentration were good choices, in the sense that they accurately represent centers of relatively high growth potential in the states. This is an extremely complex and difficult question. Any attempt to answer it involves a clear, specific definition of the objectives involved in selecting growth areas (e.g., this relates to problems of marginal versus actually growing areas, locational questions, a determination of what is desirable in terms of patterns of urban development, population and migration, etc.) and the objectives of the states have not been identical. Furthermore, this question involves the ability to quantitatively determine an area of relatively high growth potential and to compare such areas with areas of lower growth potential. The state of the art in economic theory does not allow this to be done at present. It is possible to distinguish at the extremes of a spectrum those major urban areas with the highest probability of continued economic vitality and those areas of diminishing performance whose economic future is probably bleak. However, much of Appalachia falls into the range of greater uncertainty. In fact, opinion seems to be evolving toward the view that within that relatively broad middle range of characteristics (economic and social), an area designated as having high growth potential and subsequently receiving substantial investment concentration may indeed become an area of relatively high growth. This opens up a whole new range of policy alternatives. In Chapter 8, recent events in a small number of growth centers receiving a concentration of investments are discussed, as well as general indications of the impact of those investments.

Planning and the Local Development Districts

The relationship between a state and its local development districts was never extensively elaborated by the commission. By law, these organizations must be non-profit entities certified by the state as having economic development authority. LDD's have not been created and operated in all the planning regions that constitute Appalachia. In others, where they have existed, as in West Virginia, at this writing they are being thoroughly revamped and are not operative. Consequently, generalization has to be tempered with awareness of these factors. In the following chapter, the pattern of arrangements that have developed will be examined, as well as the relationships of these LDD's to the local entities of government in their areas. At this point, where the concern is with their role in Appalachian planning, several aspects of their local and state planning relationships warrant mentioning.

Some LDD's are recognized as the local development agency by the Economic Development Administration whose law permits the establishment of analogous Economic Development Districts. EDA, like its predecessor ARA, requires the submission of an Overall Economic Development Program by its local areas as a precondition to financial support for projects. In those cases in which joint LDD-EDD's exist, these agencies have a planning responsibility not specified in the Appalachian Act or in commission requirements.

Initially, some people visualized the LDD's as becoming either successors to the multitudes of small counties in parts of the region or, at a lower level of aspiration, local technical assistance agencies. They would arrange for the provision of technical services to their member governments and prepare plans and programs for problems which go beyond the boundaries of any one jurisdiction. In a number of cases, evolution in this direction is occurring.[11]

After the passage of the Appalachian Act, Bureau of the Budget Circular A-95 was issued which requires review by a comprehensive planning agency of proposals for projects that are requesting federal funds from any agency. In some cases, states have designated LDD's to serve as the A-95 agency for their area.

In general, the role of the LDD in state planning consists of the following types of activities. First, the LDD may be asked to comment on the state's analysis of its area's problems, potentials and growth areas, or to submit its analysis for state consideration. Secondly, the LDD will frequently submit, or assist local applicants to submit, project recommendations and provide support for them. Lastly, it will frequently assist in the execution of programs when approved, particularly those of a study or planning nature.

The role of LDD's in Appalachian planning has never been particularly well defined. Reference is sometimes made to them as a fundamental building block of the regional process. They may evolve into this but they are hardly universal or universally effective in this role as of now. Later discussion will elaborate further on their role but, for now, it is sufficient to note that at present they usually serve as a vehicle for gauging local sentiment and transmitting local aspirations. Only when they have been co-extensive with the state's Appalachian area, as in South Carolina, have they been integral elements in the state planning process.

Underlying all Appalachian planning activities is the intention to use them to help accomplish social purposes, rather than have them serve as exercises for their own sake. Institutions are required to produce planning but, more importantly, they are required to implement programs to accomplish those social purposes. The ultimate test of the utility of planning is its effectiveness, and this depends as much on institutional competency as anything else. The next chapter is concerned with Appalachia's institutions and their ability to be effective instruments of social purpose.

7 Organization for Appalachian Development

When the Appalachian Regional Commission appeared on the scene, the stage was already clogged with governmental bodies, local, state and federal. Despite (or perhaps because of) their number, jurisdictions, powers and finances, Congress created another agency to coordinate, facilitate, recommend and financially support. Like the new boy on the block, the new agency had to prove itself to the more jaundiced older population of institutions. Essentially, the commission sought the attention of these governmental institutions, their cooperation in planning, and (through the implementation of the plans) the establishment of the commission's credibility as an effective agency.

Fortunately, the naive view that because Congress established an agency, others would give it more than passing notice was avoided. The pragmatic fact was accepted that usually it takes money to gain the attention of governmental agencies and other institutions. In the early stages of establishing institutional credibility, a first principle is to command attention by making funds available to further the objectives sought. Another is to go into action quickly. ARC implemented the first of these principles by the allocation formulas it devised, the second by engaging in a "quick start" period. This period covered the early months of commission operation when projects were approved at the same time that plans and project guidelines were being prepared. In this early period, project activity was deemed essential to create respect for the organization and some projects seemed so obviously desirable that conflict with later standards appeared most unlikely. The regional commissions established under the Public Works and Economic Development Act of 1965 were not given the means to operate on either of these principles, which may explain some of their lack-luster performance.

Allocation of Program Funds

A central thesis on which early operations were based, therefore, was the necessity to give the Appalachian effort in the states the funds needed to gain the attention and cooperation of the other agencies of state government. Put simply, a directive from the governor would probably not have been sufficient, or so it was believed. The means the commission used to make these funds available, allocation formulas, have been the subject of frequent notice and some searching examination. One published analysis examines them to see whether and in what sense the commission was maximizing its goals by the allocations it established.[1] Another study (by the Government Accounting Office) likens the allocation of funds to block grants, which they are not since they cannot be expended at the will of the individual state. They are more properly thought of as drawing accounts, funds available to each state but not available without strings. The "strings" consist of the submission of individual projects that pass muster when weighted against the law, the commission's criteria and the state's own plan.

The allocation formulas, which distributed the appropriated funds among the states, established the drawing account of each state. One of their purposes was to encourage intra-state cooperation which they did, though to a lesser extent than had been hoped, as part of this chapter will discuss. They also contributed a note of realism to the state's planning efforts. Without a financial planning target, each state would have been inclined to submit as many projects as possible in hopes of getting more "winners" because it had more "candidates." This would hardly have led to responsible state behavior nor would it have been useful in fostering a federal-state partnership.

Moreover, a basic question to consider is how long the commission, or any institution of its nature, would survive if each project approved for any one state decreased in funds from which all other potential projects in other states would have to be supported. Such an arrangement, with its intense competitiveness could have produced opportunities for log-rolling among the states and with the federal co-chairman. This would undoubtedly have resulted in such questionings of motives that the institution would not have been likely to survive. In those few programs for which the commission did not establish allocations of funds by formula (for example in originally implementing the health demonstrations), the problems of making inter-state comparisons of projects led to cumbersome and somewhat ineffective alternative arrangements to choose among submissions. However, the absence of allocations probably does lead to somewhat greater innovation among applicants as they strive for limited funds. It is unsettled whether these gains have been worth the cost of institutional contention or could not have been obtained by other techniques.

Basically, two systems were used to allocate appropriated funds. The first concerned only development highways.[2] The general corridor locations (and consequently each state's share of the total mileage) had been bargained out and agreed to in PARC days. The decisions made then were conditioned by a desire to fill the gaps between centers in and surrounding the region left by the Interstate and Federal Aid Primary systems. However, not enough money was available to build new mileage the full length of every corridor. A uniform adequacy rating scheme was therefore devised to evaluate the need for improvement on each section of each corridor. On the basis of these ratings, sections of highway requiring improvement were determined. Each state's share in the total cost of these became its allocation of highway funds. These allocations, plus the state's desire and ability to build mileage in its corridors, determined the amount available to it each year within the limits of the total funds available. Two of the initial states, however, received no development highway mileage. In lieu of this, Alabama and South Carolina received half of the local access mileage authorized in the same section of the act, divided on a formula basis similar to that used in other programs.

These formulas are the second, and more generally recognizable, allocative devices used by the commission. All other program funds (except for housing, local development districts, and research and demonstration) have had formulas applied to them at some time during the commission's operation. In fact, the states bear their costs of ARC operation on the basis of a similar formula. Although the weights applied differ, in each formula recognition is given to equality (equal sharing), population and area. In several, an inverse measure of per capita income appears, as well as a "need" measure if the program seemed amenable to such measurement. Specialized criteria were included in the program for land stabilization and erosion control.

These formulas have been the basis for each state's planning target and have also been the initiator of a procedure of "swaps" among the states that enable them to create a better match between fund availability in any year and their program project priorities.

The factors selected and the weights given to them resulted in a distribution of funds quite different from the one that other conceivable formulas would produce. The important question therefore is why were the formulas used selected. The answer is, quite simply, that they resulted in acceptable fund distributions. They satisfied the congressional desire that every member state be able (if it wished) to participate under every section of the act. In addition, they satisfied all those seated at the commission table as being fair and equitable. These were non-quantified considerations, based on an understanding of needs and power and on a desire to create an institution rather than destroy it with a wrangle. Quiet discussion leading to a sense of the expectations held by each state was consequently a necessary ingredient into the preparation of the set of formulas presented to the commission.

Undoubtedly, expectations and the concept of a fair and equitable distribution changed over the years, at least in some states. Occasionally, a state has indicated a desire for a review and reconsideration of the formulas. It has been quickly persuaded to desist because the resulting fracas would clearly have produced deep institutional wounds. These events are a partial answer to those who may wonder why the formulas remained unchanged as understanding and problems changed. It also counsels the most careful selection of initial allocative devices by other agencies that attempt their use because once adopted, they create expectations of percentage distributions that can only be changed by depriving some participants of "their" share.

The potential longevity of formulas of this type was emphasized in 1971.

Data from the 1970 census were available and the commission's existence had been extended for an additional four years. Despite strenuous staff efforts to devise improved formulas, the decision was finally made to retain the earlier ones, adjusting the resulting allocation only on the basis of the newer data available.

The Institutional Task

Allocation formulas were devised as a means toward accomplishing a task. Much popular emphasis has been given to the commission's economic development task but the nature of that task in institutional terms should be explicitly in mind. Achievement of the economic goals required institutional responses during the period of ARC operation. Earlier, in Chapter 3, mention was made of the problems that the burgeoning federal grant-in-aid approach had produced and of the shortcomings perceived in the earlier economic development legislation. In part, overcoming these problems and shortcomings defined the task the commission sought to do. But they did so only partially because they took no account of the structural problems widespread in state government.

The existing federal grant system was found to lack a general strategy or a coordinated approach. Its elements operated in functional isolation from each other. The commission was to develop means of coordinating functional programs among the levels of government, using its Section 214 supplemental funds, its planning requirements, its federal-state composition, and its persuasive powers.

The shortcomings of the existing economic development legislation were centered on its narrow geographic focus and its limitation to public works. The development strategy given the commission encompassed a broader geographic view and its mandate included activities in the health and education fields.

The existing grant-in-aid and economic development laws were held to underemphasize the role of the states in establishing policies and priorities. The commission structure was to provide a new route for state views to influence the allocation of federal funds and the implementation of federal policies.

In the past, program administration had led to partnership relationships being developed between federal and state agencies with similar program responsibilities. Each served as the constituency for the other, each helping the other to insulate itself from more general policy control. In the states, the problem of functional agency independence from the chief executive officer was exacerbated by the structure of state government itself, which frequently removed operating agencies from direct gubernatorial control. The commission was an attempt to remedy this also.

The federal co-chairman was to work for the coordination of federal agency programs, eliminating duplication, competition for applicants, inconsistent strategies, and unsatisfied gaps between programs. The state members of the commission, the governors or their representatives, were to combine state agency activities into a coordinated program whose strategy was to be announced and justified in the state plan and whose credibility was to be enhanced by the availability of funds directly under the control of the governor. He alone has the power to recommend a project to the commission.

State Organization

The ARDA provides virtually no guidance about state organization to accomplish the coordinative purposes expected. There is some limitation on the nature of the local development districts to be established but no mention of the structure that the states should create internally to manage their part of the task. Despite this, there has been a demonstrated need for a strong state program of planning, coordination, management and budgeting, as well as similar strengthened capabilities at the local district and local government level. Years of implementation have led the commission staff and a number of the governors to emphasize that institutional creativity is essential to the long range realization of the program's objectives. For this reason, it is important to inquire about the administrative arrangements that have characterized the states' responses to their Appalachian responsibilities and to see if any conclusions about their relative effectiveness can be discerned.

Administrative responsibility for the program has been delegated by the governors in the following patterns:

1. In Alabama, Kentucky, Tennessee and West Virginia, delegation is to a program development office or an office of federal-state relations within the executive office of the governor.

2. In Georgia and New York, responsibility resides in the state planning agency which is part of the Governor's office.

3. In Maryland, Ohio and Pennsylvania, the delegation is to a cabinet department of economic development or local affairs.

4. Mississippi's Division of Appalachian Development is a division of the governor's office related to his coordinator of federal-state programs but it is physically located in the region, not at the state capital.

5. The South Carolina Appalachian Regional Commission has program administration responsibilities. It is resident in the area it represents, the six Appalachian counties, but coordination and policy responsibility resides in an assistant to the governor who is the state representative to the federal-state Commission.

The state representative has the power to exercise the full authority of the governor as a member of the commission and, according to commission practice, he also has responsibility for setting policy and for giving the program general direction within his state. Not all state representatives become equally involved in the program, however. In some cases, this is because the governors themselves maintain different degrees of involvement. Some governors become involved in the setting of general policies, area priorities, and program and project priorities. In other states, the governor is content to concern himself solely with major policy directions, leaving other matters to his subordinates except when a "crisis" of some form or another appears. Between these extremes, there are those governors who wish to be involved not only in general policies but who also participate in decisions about priorities in general or those in specific types of major programs, such as highways or education. The degree of involvement of the governor is therefore one influence on the degree of involvement of the state representative.

Another is the extent to which the state representative is himself the head of an agency with major program implementation responsibilities. If he is a governor's assistant, with a broad range of other responsibilities, the tendency is to delegate administration and implementation of the program and focus on major policies, as would be expected. If the state representative is head of an office of federal-state relations, or a similar agency, he tends to concern himself with more aspects of the program. The same is true of those representatives who head Appalachian units in other state agencies or who head other cabinet level departments.

Although it might seem that more intimate involvement of the representative in administration and implementation rather than merely in major policy issues would be more desirable, this is not necessarily the case. Greater degrees of involvement have been coupled usually with greater remoteness from the governor. This has two inhibiting effects.

Remoteness from the governor means that the state representative has the position of one among equals when he attempts to focus state policy on Appalachian objectives. In dealing with other agencies of the state, his Appalachian status gives him no special power to achieve the degree of coordination and complementarity of programs that the overall effort seeks. Moreover, it means that the governor is probably not taking full advantage of the opportunity the program was to give him. One of the typical problems of a governor is having state agency bureaucracies which are not fully responsive to him. The direct availability to him of the funds from ARC was intended, in part, to give him a means of widening his control over state priorities, policies and programs. He does not take full advantage of this opportunity if program administration is quite remote from him. Surely, in some cases, the governors have not capitalized on this opportunity because they failed to perceive it, or because they were not concerned with the issue, or because they perceived better routes to the same objective. In addition, in some states, the relatively small sums involved in the Appalachian program and the relatively small proportion of the state's territory and population involved militated against using the Appalachian program to widen gubernatorial control. In some state administrations, on the other hand, despite small sums and relatively minor territorial involvement, the Appalachian effort has been a means used by a governor to place his imprint on the entire range of state government.

The second inhibiting effect stemming from remoteness of the state representative from his governor has been his inability to speak in the name of the governor. Internal commission policy debate and decisions have been delayed repeatedly because those at the commission table could not speak for their governor. In some cases, it is even doubtful if individual representatives had many, or any, opportunities to speak with their governor. They had to seek guidance on policy issues by sending them up through the chain of command till they reached someone who could decide (the governor or someone close to him). This left the representative uncertain whether the issue had been decided in the full context in which he perceived it. He would also have no perception of the degree of flexibility that existed in the state's position. Without this, he would have difficulty becoming an active force for accommodation of diverse views within the commission, since he might not know precisely which of his state's purposes were to be served by the position adopted. This also damaged the effectiveness of the commission in its relations with federal agencies. To the degree that the representatives of the governors are remote from them, to that same degree executive and legislative agencies of the federal government are inclined to discount the commission as an effective mechanism to obtain an authoritative statement of a blended federal-state point of view.

All the considerations enumerated would lead to support of the idea of having a state representative whose place in the state's administrative hierarchy was reasonably close to the governor. However, governor's offices are not designed, nor should they necessarily be, to become involved in the detailed planning and implementation aspects of program administration. A compromise that will probably be unsatisfactory in some respects is required, the nature of which is probably unique to each state and the personality of each administration. Two principles seem to warrant universal acceptance, however. The first is that policy and program development should be intimately related to the planning that provides its foundation. The second is that the projects recommended should be logically related to the planning and policy and program decisions. The way in which the states have discharged their Appalachian responsibilities has not always left these principles unviolated.

Effectiveness of State Planning

Ideally, a state plan should be the joint product of a state's technical and policy staffs. It should be an integrated document that includes descriptions and analyses, logically derived policies and program priorities, and the projects that are expected to contribute most to achieving them. To be fully useful, it should be a statement of major policy importance. It should warrant being viewed by executive and legislative agencies as a statement of administration evaluation and intention, analogously to the way in which a budget should be treated. These objectives are not likely to be fully achieved if the components of a state plan are prepared separately, at different times and by different groups.

The decision in the early months of the commission's operation to require a state plan left many of the member states without the capability of preparing one. For some the concept of planning was alien, with hobgoblin implications. For others, the fears were absent, but so was the capacity to respond. In others, planning agencies existed but they had traditionally been so remote from substantive effects on policy that the thought of their intimate involvement was frightening to them and to those with policy responsibilities. In still others, a useful planning group existed with the necessary degree of competence and acceptability to do the job. All states agreed, as witnessed by their unanimous votes, that the preparation of a plan was a logically necessary step in their participation. But their situations dictated a variety of means of accomplishing it.

For the plan to be a statement of state policy, involvement of the state representative and his staff is clearly mandatory and to one degree or another (in some states, in some years, to a small degree) this was achieved. The actual preparation of the first plan submitted, however, was not done by state personnel in the majority of cases. In more than half the states, the bulk of the initial plan was produced by state university personnel, private consultants under contract, or commission personnel loaned to the state. Though no longer the majority group, six states still obtain substantial outside intellectual support in preparing their plans. Apparently, the initial decision to seek help outside the state government set a pattern that has been difficult to reverse despite the apparent wisdom of doing so. In these states, the perception of the state's Appalachian area gained during plan preparation is lost to the day-to-day administration of the program, and the plan itself tends to consist of poorly connected components, produced by different groups, remote from each other. In only four states is the entire plan produced by the states' Appalachian staff.

The pattern that has evolved has tended to produce planning documents with a strong emphasis on the description and analysis of resources, and social and economic factors. In part, this is desirable and was furthered by the commission staff who work with the states during the preparatory stages and who have the responsibility of providing reviews of the documents filed. In part, this was the logical route that an outsider to state government would choose. Being removed from policy setting and program determination, he would seek to discharge his contract with exhaustive treatment of these seemingly less policy sensitive resource, social and economic factors. The problem that developed is that the transition from this treatment of the anatomy of the entire area, to the treatment given to the sub-parts of the area, to the selection of policies, programs, and projects was not as conceptually tightly linked as might be feasible. Of course, setting policies and program and project priorities is not a purely technical matter. There should be a dominant role for officials directly responsible to the electorate. Moreover, there is no unambiguous technical link between analyses of the sort included in the state plans and these policy decisions. Still, the documents do not reflect as complete use of the analyses they contain as might have been feasible for illuminating the options available for decision and their implications.

The policy decisions that are reflected in the plans relate to the delineation of areas with growth potential and to the programs to be emphasized, since these are basic reflections of state policy. For example, to what extent does the state seek to rejuvenate decaying urban centers and to what extent does it seek to influence the pattern of urban growth into other, less urbanized areas? To what extent will it emphasize consumer travel time reduction as a means of delivering services rather than the development of satellite, mobile and other out-reach facilities to widen the availability of health and education services? To what extent will it seek to foster economic expansion through industrially related investments (for example, access roads to industrial parks) or will it emphasize investments leading directly to improved health service availability and education levels? These are decisions that are related intimately to analysis but if the people who make the decisions are not in intimate communication with those who make the analyses, it is unlikely that the analyses prepared will be relevant to the questions that need to be resolved. Regrettably, the continued remoteness of those charged with the analytical component of the plan from those making policy decisions does not suggest that rapid improvement is likely.

Since the analytical component of the state plans is frequently somewhat remote from its policy and program components, project recommendations logically tend to be somewhat remote from them also. Proposals for projects come to a state's Appalachian office from a variety of sources—local groups and governments, local development districts, and state agencies being the most frequent ones. In addition, projects may be initiated by the staff of the office itself, based upon their perceptions and their sense of receptivity among others to the idea. The list that is developed is always greater than can be recommended, for a variety of reasons. Policy constraints at the state or ARC level eliminate some; the unavailability of federal program funds, others; insufficient local financial support or state financial support weeds out others; a relative shortage of Appalachian funds eliminates still others; some clearly fall beyond the program emphases the state has adopted. The process of rejecting a proposal at the state level is not a simple one, however, because several agencies and interests may be inter-mixed in each one, requiring effort to discern all the issues and potentials that are involved. Frequently, a long negotiative phase may be involved as the scope, impact and merits of projects are weighed and sponsors gradually encouraged or discouraged from pressing their preferences. Finally, a list of recommended projects is devised which receives a policy-level review, possible alteration, and affirmation before being sent to the commission as the state's package of recommended projects for the ensuring period, usually a year.

Both technical and policy considerations are elements of this process, with the various factors receiving different and sometimes fluctuating weights. No matter how strong the analytical base which exists for the policy and program emphasis of the state, it would be easy to loosen its discipline in the project selection process and revert solely to more typical criteria of selection—physical capability and political desirability. The state plans which lack a strong conceptual link between analysis and policy are more likely to be prey to this reversion. The tendency has been least apparent in those cases in which plan preparation and program responsibility reside in the same agency. The logic of integration of plan components that lay behind the commission requirements is apparent in that setting, seemingly, and the mechanisms for achieving it are also present.

Despite the pitfalls that the Appalachian experience has made evident so far, the picture is not all bleak. At worst, the state plans could have been written after the selection of projects as a rationalizing document that reversed the intended logic. There is no external evidence or evidence internal to the plans that suggests this occurred. Moreover, there is evidence of serious attempts to devise analytical techniques that are useful for program decision purposes. In some states, sincere and somewhat successful attempts have been made to use the plan's analyses as important contributants to policy decisions. For some states, the experience in Appalachian planning has proven to be a stimulus to a more generalized application of the approach to the state in general and to state programs in general. For these states, there can be some hope that the ultimate institutional goal of a focused, harmonious state government working toward specified goals can be achieved.

Overall, the plan requirements of the commission have not been useless, "window-dressing" exercises that must be accomplished, like a rite of passage, to gain access to the federal treasury. The extent to which they are more than this is intimately related to the way the state chooses among its option. If it sets out to create a strong management tool at the center of state government that can achieve improved coordination of state and federal efforts, it can have that effect. If it separates the various components of the plan among different groups, less than this is achieved and there is ultimately a tendency to administer the program through one or more functional agencies where it is viewed as merely one more source of money to do things related to their other, usually narrow, objectives. In keeping with its overall orientation, the program would be better served by the former approach than the latter.

It is a knotty question, however, how the commission can influence or set requirements for the pattern of state administration (other than by staff persuasion or persuasion by the States' regional representative). The states are reluctant to imply criticism of each other and the concept of a federal-state partnership of equality inhibits strong federal pressure on the subject. In addition, the federal government's structure is hardly in such order that the defensive reply of "heal thyself" might not properly be made.

In its early years, the commission provided financial support to the states for the purpose of assisting them in the process of getting organized to discharge their Appalachian responsibilities. Experience now suggests that greater efforts to influence the pattern of organization might have had very useful later results. However, at that point, the implications of alternative structures were not at all as well perceived as they now are. And the commission had yet to establish credibility as an effective agency, a precondition for ready acceptance of its proposals. In effect, when the opportunity may have existed, neither the wisdom nor the credibility required were present. Now the task is to find means and methods to that end.

The importance of the end is hard to overstate. It is not merely a belief that good governmental management requires coordinated actions toward accepted goals. More fundamentally, it is important because the resources needed to help Appalachians toward the twin goals of growth and development are likely always to be harshly scarce relative to the need for them. Careful husbanding of them and their joint use with funds from all other sources is required. To achieve that requires a plan like those sought by the commission. And to achieve such a plan requires the appropriate organization of state government. Fortunately, the planning and structure for planning that exist in the Appalachian states have evolved to the point where examples of coordinated actions are numerous. In the next chapter, activities in various functional areas will be discussed but note can be taken here of some examples:

1. Alteration of highway department criteria in selecting sections and routes for improvement to include development criteria in addition to traditional traffic counts,
2. Joint funding by several federal, state and local agencies and groups of the acquisition of land, its improvement and the provision of access to it for public purposes, such as an industrial park,
3. Access road construction that makes feasible the development of housing or schools or health facilities,
4. Provision of the health services that are needed in an area to enable it to host certain industrial activities,
5. Land reclamation programs integrated with urban renewal, recreation, and education developments,
6. Water resource projects developed as necessary parts of urban renewal and model city projects.
7. Designing borrow and fill sites needed in public facility construction so that developable sites result.

Local Development Districts[3]

During the early period when the commission was partially financing the operation of the states' activities in the program, one of the tasks to be accomplished was the organization of their approach to local development districts. In retrospect, it now appears that there may have been another opportunity at that point that was not fully perceived or grasped. Whether or not this view is taken will depend markedly upon the concept of a development district adopted. Such variety has evolved within the region that numerous alternatives are now present and in some areas, development district organizations have not yet appeared.

Any discussion of the way the states implemented the local development district (LDD) aspect of the Appalachian program must be placed in a context that specifies the multitude of local districts that have been required or stimulated by federal legislation. In addition to the Soil Conservation Services' Resource Conservation and Development Districts, stimulation has been given to local development districts, and economic development districts, all three of which have rather broad ranges of interest. Broad interests are evident also in the community action agencies, metropolitan planning districts, and non-metropolitan planning districts. More specific focuses exist for comprehensive area health planning districts, law enforcement planning agencies, area transportation planning councils, cooperative area manpower planning systems boards, watershed and flood protection districts, and so forth. Though some of these agencies have a long history, in the past decade federal legislation and regulations have stimulated such a proliferation of local boards with overlapping jurisdictions and memberships that order was clearly required. This was sought through a series of presidential actions, beginning with a 1966 memorandum to federal agencies requiring them to coordinate their efforts so that conflict and duplication among local groups receiving federal support would be minimized. There followed two Budget Circulars (A-80 and A-95) which required first that procedures to achieve this be instituted and secondly (as mentioned earlier) that projects to receive federal support be reviewed by clearing house agencies.

In this welter of required or permitted local organizations, the appearance of the possibility of support for LDD's injected complication as well as opportunity. No one was precisely certain how to proceed and the legislative history provided less than clear guidance. The LDD had originally been conceived as the local counterpart of a regional development corporation which could make funds available to local interests for needed investments. When the regional corporation idea was excised, the funding function of the local organization went with it and the remaining structure became the nucleus of the LDD. The only important certainties that existed were that they were to be agencies created by the states; to be multi-county and multi-purpose but not operate functional programs; to be professionally staffed but have representation of local groups as well as governments on their boards; to be related (in partially undefined ways) to the analysis, priority and program decisions of the overall program; and, hopefully, to build upon existing institutions and capabilities, rather than duplicating them.

In common with many states in the union, some Appalachian states have responded to the multiplicity of federally stimulated districts with the passage of laws establishing statewide systems of planning and development districts that serve as wide a range as possible of local, state and federal programs. In addition to this general stimulus, the Appalachian states had the additional incentive provided by the language of the LDD section of the act and the funding it permitted. At this writing, six Appalachian states (Alabama, Georgia, Kentucky, South Carolina, Tennessee and Virginia) have a statewide system of planning districts and have created organizations in them to serve as coordinators of local efforts to take advantage of state, regional and national programs. Four more states in the region (New York, North Carolina, Pennsylvania and West Virginia) have established a consistent set of boundaries for these planning districts but have not set up organizations in all of them whose boundaries conform to the planning boundaries. (West Virginia is reorganizing all its districts.) Only Maryland, Mississippi, and Ohio have taken neither step.

In this setting, the commission code is highly general in dealing with the functional characteristics of the LDD. In summary, it provides that:

— the districts are to have a full-time staff, directly responsible to the chief administrator, of sufficient professional competence to plan, coordinate, and administer an Appalachian development program;
— the professional-level staffs are to meet written employee qualification standards approved by the state representative and the commission;
— the states are to provide for coordination of LDD support grants with planning grants authorized for economic development districts and, where appropriate, to combine the grants;
— the districts are to coordinate planning efforts under other federal, state, and local laws providing assistance for regional, state, and local planning;
— and in conformity with the law, 25% of the operating costs are to come from non-federal sources.

To give the states time to formulate their LDD program, the commission established each state as an LDD for a maximum three-year period, during which the format of local structures was to be created. Whatever other benefits this may have had, it served to delay the establishment of truly local LDD's so that the full effect of the district program was delayed by up to three years. It is a moot question, however, whether a shortening of the state-wide LDD period would have accelerated markedly the creation of the local organizations since enabling legislation was required in several states, some of which had legislatures that met only every other year. In those states, the technical and political preparation needed before legislative presentation probably would have precluded a more compressed schedule.

Generally speaking, the existing 54 districts[4] are operating under three different legal arrangements. Most are regional planning agencies established by state statute. Others operate as councils of governments under the state's non-profit corporation enabling legislation, or they operate under similar laws but not as councils of government.

Whatever their precise legal status, if an LDD is to be effective, it has to deal effectively with the local powers-that-be. Generally, their governing boards consist of *ex officio* members (who hold their seats because of their elected positions in local government) and of appointive members, typically chosen by those same units of government. They are likely therefore to be representative of the local district in the same sense that any elected official is representative of his constituency.

One virtue of this membership structure is that the common meeting ground of the LDD board room tends to engender the understanding and cooperation among the leaders of separate local governments that is central to the idea of a regional approach. An offset is the loss of other perspectives and priorities that could come from boards with different compositions.

Another virtue of the membership structure is that it tends to make less difficult the acquisition of the local funds needed to finance the LDD's. Non-federal support is required for 25% of the costs and only in Alabama, Georgia, Kentucky, Pennsylvania, Tennessee and Virginia do the states themselves make any contribution. The rest must come from local sources. A mark of the effectiveness of the LDD's in combining federal funding sources is that in 1970 more than half the districts received federal funds from one or more agencies other than ARC (a total of seven federal agencies were involved). In fact, in 20% of the districts, more federal funds came from agencies other than ARC than from the commission.

This funding pattern is an indication that the concept of the LDD as a comprehensive organization, capable of bringing a range of program opportunities to bear on local issues may be in the process of being realized. A widely distributed pattern of funding sources is indicative of alertness but it has inherent in it potential conflict also. The federal funds do not come with a consistent philosophy or concept of local agency purposes or functions. It may be that multiple funding, producing multiple masters, can inhibit the creation of a consistent analysis and strategy to underpin local programs. Eighty percent of the LDD's are so dependent on ARC funding that this may not yet be a problem, but as the likely ultimate disappearance of ARC as a source of support becomes more imminent, they will probably seek other sources of support and adopt the attitudes and approaches required by them. The commission's convictions about the appropriateness of its approach should be mirrored therefore in efforts to create permanent, sympathetic sources of funding. The fact that six states already provide some financial support and that three more, while not doing so have permissive legislation, is a hopeful sign.

To warrant support, the districts should be engaged in activities that their sponsors deem useful. On the average, the single most time-consuming activity of the districts' staffs is district-wide planning and research. Almost a third of the average LDD's staff time is devoted to this. These do not usually tend to be efforts devoted to developing a comprehensive, multifunctional plan for the district. For reasons discussed in the preceding chapter, planning of this type is not always the most useful variety, though in some situations it is certainly warranted, and is occurring in less than 10% of the LDD's. In the rest of the LDD's, the research and planning tends to place more emphasis on gathering data on the district and preparing district-wide or sub-district functional plans, dealing usually with obvious deficiencies in physical infrastructure, such as roads, water and sewer systems, education, health, etc. District-wide planning of another type occurs in those LDD's which also receive funding from the Economic Development Administration. These occasionally are involved in the preparation and updating for the Overall Economic Development Program required by EDA.

The next most important LDD function, measured by staff time devoted to it, tends to be activities related to developing and reviewing grant proposals—the relatively new American expertise of grantsmanship. These activities cover the range from idea generation to support stimulation, project application and review and (finally) proposal prodding in the state and federal agencies through which the paper passes. Very little staff time is devoted to activities following project approval. The LDD's are not administering agencies. That function is typically conducted by other local units. However, LDD staffs could conceivably devote some time to analyses of the impact of completed projects, particularly as the inventory of these expands. Thus far, no state has concertedly prodded them in this direction, nor has the commission.

The grantsmanship function of the LDD should not be minimized. To gain their own credibility, they have to "bring home the bacon." But in doing so, they fill a void that is particularly present in under-urbanized Appalachia. The region has had a paucity of professional and full-time public servants to keep the area informed of its opportunities and the processes that must be followed to capitalize on them. The LDD is designed to help fill this void and it is therefore not a passive conduit of projects, when its job is done properly. It is the advisor and initiator and technical staff for the local units as well.

Closely related to the grantsmanship role, therefore, is the next most important consumer of the staffs' energies—providing technical services to local government units and providing public information. Administrative functions and (for those with that responsibility) reviews required to discharge the obligations under Circular A-95 largely consume the balance of the time available.

The difficulty with the preceding discussion is that it is based on averages and therefore lumps together districts with a staff of a director and a secretary with those that have professional staffs of ten or more.[5] Another difficulty with the discussion of an "average" LDD's activities is that they are not homogeneous in other ways. They are the creations and creatures of the states which have given them different structures, authorities and responsibilities. The averages therefore mask these interstate differences.

Despite the hazards of generalized discussion, however, it is possible to summarize LDD activities as falling primarily into the areas indicated. If any trend is discernible in their activities, it is in the direction of greater participation in local activities and a closer relationship to the states' activities. In some fields, the LDD's have displayed considerable initiative in the development of new programs, which when presented to state officials have led them to support them on a demonstration basis, and sometimes to ultimately include them in the priority items on the state's agenda. This has been true in fields such as solid waste disposal, housing, and youth and regional educational service agency development. The districts have become more involved in not merely transmitting proposals to the state but in ranking them by local criteria to serve as a contributor to the state's ranking process.

The LDD program is too new for firm conclusions about it to be reached and the lack of complete coverage of the counties in the region weakens conclusions still further. Experience makes it logical to suppose, however, that the LDD's are in that early phase of credibility establishment that requires a heavy project and functional program orientation. This may provide the groundwork for an expanded range of activities that may achieve the planning and priority establishing role that is potentially present. As previously mentioned, some have thought it possible that in some parts of the region LDD's might someday become successors to the excess of small governmental units in their areas. That day is far off but they may become the agency through which inter-governmental cooperation and sharing of professional talent and public facilities will increasingly emerge.

ARC's Effectiveness with Federal Agencies

If the purposes of the Appalachian undertaking were to be served, the states would have to effectively marshall their resources; the local development districts would have to meld local interests into a strategy and program; and the federal government would have to coordinate and focus its resources and agencies on the region's problems and potentials. The federal government has not been notably successful in coordinating its functions and agencies in any area and it is no surprise, therefore that the ARC, with limited funds and limited life, was not able to prod it to do much better. Judgment of the degree of success achieved has to be a blending of those cases in which virtually no successes existed, such as the case of the FAA mentioned in Chapter 6, and those in which highly cooperative relationships were developed, as with the Federal Highway Administration.

Generally speaking, the commission has been able to obtain the full cooperation of an agency when it entered into an agreement with that agency to administer specified aspects of a program created or expanded under the Appalachian Act. For example, the Department of Agriculture discharges most of the administrative functions, under commission guidance, for the land stabilization, erosion control and conservation program. Comparable arrangements exist in the highway field and with the Office of Education in vocational education. There have been exceptions even in these more harmonious relationships but generally they have been satisfactory. However, this is not what is commonly meant by inter-agency coordination and cooperation. What is usually intended is not the agreed distribution of administrative responsibilities. Rather, the intention is to achieve common strategies and complementary focusing of programs. Examples of this exist in individual cases, at individual locations or on individual prominent problems. An example might be the aftermath of the collapse of the Silver Bridge over the Ohio River in 1967, or forestalling the imminent financial collapse of the system of Miners Hospitals in the central part of the region, or the focusing of agency programs on a particular development opportunity of a new industrial park in Virginia or a model city in Kentucky. These cases demonstrate that it can be done but their exceptional character indicates that fundamental inhibitions must exist to make such cases relatively rare. A review of the commission's experiences dealing with some agencies can highlight some of the reasons for rarity.[6]

The later 1960's had more than their quota of coordinating committees among agencies in Washington. Appalachia was centrally involved in two of them, the Federal Development Planning Committee for Appalachia that filled the interval between the termination of PARC and the passage of the act, and the Federal Development Committee for Appalachia. The latter was created after the act's passage as the means for coordination and consultation by the federal co-chairman with appropriate agencies before casting his ballot on the commission. These two committees, like their counterparts throughout the government, were not useful devices. The chairman, who was the ARC co-chairman, the one charged with coordinating everyone, was one among equals, a situation that duplicated the experience earlier discussed at the state level. He lacked any "muscle" in any form to encourage cooperation and particularly, the form that would have been most useful, the ability to alter the basic instructions to an agency. That is the crucial one because most frequently, the agencies charged to cooperate have been given other inconsistent charges by Congress. With the best of wills, coordination in the face of inconsistent legal instructions would be difficult. Moreover, the decisions made by agencies as they implement their instructions lead to rules and regulations tailored to the situation of the particular part of the public they think they principally serve. Compromise among conflicting publics through executive agencies reflecting these different interests, grounded on noncompatible legislative instructions, is more than any muscle-less coordinating committee can achieve. Appalachia's were no exception.

The decision during the days of PARC's operation to shift human resources programs needed in the region to the nascent poverty program dictated a strong motivation toward cooperation between the ARC and the Office of Economic Opportunity (OEO), the agency that had been created in 1964 to administer the War on Poverty. The early history augured well. The federal co-chairman was made a member of the Economic Opportunity Council of OEO which was their agency for achieving coordination and the director of OEO sat on the ARC counterpart. To obtain closer coordination, individual contacts between the federal co-chairman and OEO's director were initiated and staff contacts were established, some of which have continued fruitfully, particularly in the field of data distribution. In these first months, OEO funding of commission sponsored projects in the health field was received. Before long, however, difficulties appeared which ultimately led to a several year long period of walking separate paths.

With a common interest in improving the lot of those in distress and a common background in the concerns that led to the establishment of PARC, the schism that appeared may seem surprising but basic differences of legislation and orientation made it probably inescapable.

Most basically, the commission program was grounded on the belief that progress could be made by working through and with the established centers of political and economic power. Hence, the orientation toward state and local government involvement and the anticipation of private employment growth as a remedy to many of the problems of the people of the region. OEO, on the other hand, operated on a supposition that the power structure was the problem and not the route to its alleviation. The most obvious manifestation was its insistence on vigorous interpretation of the words in its law requiring "maximum feasible participation" of the poor. However, throughout the organization there was ill-concealed, and sometimes revealed, hostility toward those groups through which the commission was trying to work. In implicit and explicit ways, coordination was damaged as a result.

One of the explicit ways was the unsuccessful attempt by the commission to achieve common local organizations. Both OEO and ARC were trying to organize their local bodies, the OEO's Community Action Agencies (CAAs) and ARC's LDD's. In Appalachia, which had such a dearth of leadership anyway, it seemed to ARC unwise to try to establish two sets of organizations, especially since in the setting of the region, overlapping memberships were likely. (ARC included in its desired coordination the EDD's being established by EDA, but more on that later). OEO was dubious that the wishes of the poor and the priority ranking of the services they desired would come from the type of organization ARC would find compatible. OEO anticipated that ARC sponsored groups would be more likely to emphasize simply economic development, and not necessarily even those forms of economic development most compatible with the needs and desires of the poor. Though OEO never forbade the creation of joint local groups, their universal absence speaks for itself.

It might be argued that two agencies serving the same constituency but in different ways may be better able to conduct their work through separate local groups. This may well be true and be the efficient decision. However, in the case of Appalachia, the lack of cooperation has been costly. On occasion, it produced inconsistent programs between the agencies that may be disadvantageous to the people both seek to assist.

ARC's emphasis has been on creating conditions leading to the appearance of new jobs in the region but not necessarily in a pattern that would be compatible with the present population distribution. Implicit in its growth strategy, its emphasis on urbanization and on the growth of urban-type service employment, has been the anticipation that population redistribution would occur within the region. An impediment to this redistribution, in the commission's view, was any program that tended to encourage the people to remain geographically located in places that made it difficult to bring services to them or from which it was unlikely they could commute to employment. OEO sponsorship of programs in the most remote hollows that could reduce the incentive to migrate, though defensible on humanitarian grounds, brought questioning from the commission. Essentially, the question was, is this in the long run interest of the people being served. Obviously, from their different vantage points and philosophies (which are grounded in their basic legislation) the agencies gave different responses. It is impossible at this point to assert which is necessarily correct. It is possible to see how far cooperation among agencies can go, faced with such a disagreement.

Before ARC was a year old, relations between it and OEO had cooled and quieted. Attempts at cooperation were largely dropped, with ARC expressing an anticipation that greater degrees of cooperation could be achieved at the state and local level. This proved unwarranted, for much the same reasons that success had not been achieved in Washington. The history of the attempts by governors and mayors throughout the country to gain increasing control over funds made available to their areas by OEO is witness to the feelings that officials in the Appalachian area generally shared.

If cooperation between OEO and ARC foundered largely because of inconsistent philosophies, the fate of cooperation between ARC and the Economic Development Administration might be expected to have been more fruitful. Unfortunately, this was not the case either, though for very different reasons since the two did share similar orientations.

Historically, both ARC and EDA came into being in 1965. Both grew out of the experience with ARA that was discussed in Chapter 3. Parts of the Public Works and Economic Development Act which created EDA were a response to demands that the special treatment provided for Appalachia be made available to other regions. This was the origin of Title V of the PWEDA and the regional action commissions created under it. Both are influenced, though in different degrees, by the growth area idea. Under the Appalachian Act, these were to be the focus of the investment strategy. Under EDA's legislation, investments in "economic development centers" were permitted if it could be expected that they would significantly assist nearby areas of distress in the same development district. Obviously, both were intended to eliminate economic distress and both were to operate through public works, with the aim of increasing private employment.

These would all seem to be sufficient preconditions for cooperation but there was one more important one. The authorization for EDA contained half a billion dollars a year. Since Appalachia could hope to get roughly one third of this (the region had about one-third of the eligible areas), combining the resources of the two agencies in their approach to the region would have substantially expanded the potential impact. EDA had certain program authorities that ARC lacked which would have been permitted some divisions of labor that would allow each to maintain institutional identity.

The unsuccessful attempts at cooperation can be explained by three factors. One is an administrative arrangement that is no longer operative but that left a residue of strained relations that is only now virtually dissipated. The other two, issues of constituency and strategy, remain and continue to dim prospects for a coordinated approach.

The administrative arrangement that damaged inter-agency relations arose from the fact that prior to June of 1967, ARC did not, in fact, approve projects that were to be funded by appropriations under its enabling act. Rather, ARC recommended approval to existing federal agencies. For some significant sections of the act, for example highways, supplemental grants, and development district, research and demonstration grants, the operating agency was the Department of Commerce. For the latter two types of grants mentioned, Commerce delegated its authority to an Appalachian Office of EDA. Relations between that office and ARC were not good. From the standpoint of ARC, the functions of the office should have been routine since all proposals had been scrutinized by commission staff. The ARC position was that virtually a rubber stamp should have been enough, rather than a review staff larger than the commission's. EDA took its responsibilities far more seriously and, though the issue never came to a head, adopted the view that it could reject a commission recommendation, if it interpreted the Appalachian Act to preclude the action. Regardless of the merits of the arguments, and they were made moot when authority to approve projects was granted the commission in 1967, their existence clouded relationships at the policy level. And they did equal damage at the staff level.

Although it may not be immediately apparent, the constituencies of the two agencies are somewhat different, despite the similarity of objectives. EDA shared with OEO the view that their constituents were local groups, not the state governments. Projects came to EDA through its field offices, not the governors' offices. The field staff of EDA served to bring its program to local groups and to counsel and advise them (as the state staffs did under ARC) but without necessarily being concerned with the policy and priority guidance of the state. EDA found it difficult to accept the idea that strategies adopted by the state should persuasively influence its investment decisions when it was funding and accepting Overall Economic Development Programs which might not conform to the state's views. ARC felt it was constrained by law to work through the states and on the basis of their priorities. It argued that the local views were likely to be parochial and that uncoordinated policies from individual districts or counties would lead to inefficient patterns of expenditure.

The other basic impediment to cooperation was the investment strategy each agency adopted. Appalachia's was one of concentration in areas of significant growth potential. EDA's was one of dispersal. At one point, over a thousand counties were eligible for EDA assistance and it had no legislated criterion to reduce the dispersion this would create. When they tried to create one, they chose the policy of "worst-first," a policy of giving greater entitlement to EDA funds, the greater the area's measure of distress, such as high unemployment or low per capita income. Though never fully implemented, the worst-first policy logically lead to highest priority for areas with limited or no growth potential at all. On the basis of such a policy position, cooperation between the agencies was not possible. Moreover, the staff of each agency thought the other's strategy so misguided that the intellectual basis of respect needed for cooperation was eroded.

The net effect of these factors was a period of uncoordinated activity. One unfortunate by-product of this period (among many) was that it gave the Appalachian states a means to mollify those communities whose projects they would or could not recommend to ARC. These local groups were given the advice to "see if you can't get the money from EDA." Frequently, they could.

At the staff level, cooperation between the two agencies improved slowly after 1967. Data and information services have been shared and project applications are now flowing between EDA and ARC for staff comments. As previously indicated, joint funding of development districts is occurring and agreements have been reached under which EDA will fund no district that intersects two or more Appalachian LDD's.

There is emerging evidence that a period of greater, though possibly not great, cooperation may be coming. EDA is looking again at the section of its act that allows it to take a growth center approach in its investment strategy. Independently, it is designating growth centers in Appalachia, which conform to those in state plans better than 90% of the time. If these designations are followed by similar emphasis in allocations, significant cooperation may be possible. However, the differing nature of the institutions will still exist. ARC is a joint agency and it can logically vest a significant portion of its investment decisions in the states. EDA is a federal agency. It must take full responsibility for the funds appropriated to it since its act does not contain a basis for sharing responsibility. That institutional difference, plus the lack of full compatibility in area eligibility, makes intimate cooperation unlikely no matter how relationships improve. What should be possible is for the two agencies to develop a priority system that allows each to give special consideration to projects in areas eligible under both acts and which conform to both EDD and state priorities and strategies.

After the experiences it had had with coordinating committees, and with OEO and EDA, it is understandable that the ARC was reluctant to engage in many attempts to carry out its mandate to review federal programs and make recommendations for changes to enhance their effectiveness in the region. The internal assessment of the probability of success was so low that devoting time to these activities received a lower priority than the seemingly more pressing obligation to initiate programs explicitly authorized by the act. The jaundiced, but perhaps frequently accurate view was adopted that other agencies, operating under other laws and other priority systems, answerable to other constituencies and congressional committees would look askance at inquiry and recommendations from an untried agency. It was even uncertain whether the federal-state nature of the commission would be a help or hindrance. To be neutral is one thing, to be a eunuch is another.

Despite reluctances and uncertainties about involvements with federal agencies, the commission has had an impact on national programs in housing and in education and is likely to have a similarly beneficial effect in early childhood development. Events in these areas fall more properly into the following chapter but here, one common attribute of all three areas should be noted. In all three, the commission initially had no operating program (other than facility construction of education). What it did have were some energetic staff people, interested in the program and in these aspects of a potential program, who were sufficiently free of operating responsibilities that they could discharge the obligation given to all professional employees—to delve into existing programs to find how they can be used or altered to serve the interests of the people of the region better.

It might appear to follow from this that the number of successful cases would have been larger had the professional staff been larger, so that freedom from operating responsibilities would have brought inquiry and recommendations in a wider range of fields. This might be true but it assumes that the requisite people would have been available had the employment opportunities been made available. That is unknowable. There are grounds to speculate, however, that if the decision had not been made to severely limit the size of the staff, programmatic entrepreneurship might have been more common. To offset this, however, large organizations produce their own rigidities and inhibitions.

If speculation is all that is possible on the effects of staff size on the regional program, it is also all that is possible concerning another aspect of commission operation. Mention was made earlier in this chapter that ARC's task in dealing with federal agencies was made more difficult to the extent that the states' internal organization was not as effective as possible. A question can be raised about whether or not their performance may not have resulted, in part, from the commission's internal organization.

As described in Chapter 2, the commission's day-to-day policy operations are the responsibility of the executive committee whose voting members are the federal co-chairman and the states' regional representative (SRR) who serves for all the states. There is some reason to believe that the effect of the executive committee device may have been to make the individual states somewhat remote from the consideration of policy alternatives and implementation of policy. Operations and decisions proceeded rather smoothly so there may not have appeared to be a need for the states to allocate scarce, high-level time of the governor or an important assistant to the program. The perverse may have occurred. Without the executive committee device there may have been an overt need for greater state involvement that might have precipitated more effective organizational patterns internal to the states, the subject with which this chapter began. Or is it possible that without the functioning of the executive committee, the states would have had no equally effective means to address policy issues and the commission would have become a facade for federal policy-making?

Not only are these questions speculative because there is no substantial body of evidence from alternative structures for comparison purposes, but the results in ARC's experience are reflections of both individual personalities and of institutions, inter-mixed in partially indistinguishable ways. The same is true of the entire prior discussion of institutions in this chapter. In generalizing about what was done and how it might have been done better, it is impossible to separate out totally the influence of individuals from that of institutions. All that can be done is to study, speculate and, if it seems warranted, innovate.

8

Program Expenditures for Appalachian Development

The preceding pages are filled with comments about the criteria for various investment programs and their backgrounds. None of these functional programs has yet been described in detail. That is the task of this chapter. It consists of a series of individual sections, each devoted to a program or set of programs, designed to highlight operating experience with them.

Approaching the subject in this manner only permits examination of such questions as how much was invested in how many projects and whether they have been operating as expected. These are surely of interest but there are other important questions too. A program-by-program approach cannot examine the extent to which the commission succeeded in concentrating its investments as was intended. This treatment provides no scope for the synergistic effects of programs which are disparate in nature but all affecting a limited area and its population. The thesis of the Appalachian approach is that their interactive effects will be greater than the sum of the parts, a thesis that the program-by-program treatment in this chapter makes it difficult to examine. The following chapter, Chapter 9, will attempt to remedy these inadequacies by addressing the issues of project concentration and synergistic effects, among others. Before they can be tackled, however, insight into the functional programs is necessary.

Highways and Access Roads

One of the more common descriptions of the Appalachian program, and one that is usually expressed critically, is that it is basically a highway program. This is an impression and description that probably finds some of its basis in the original legislation, which provided $840 million, a lion's share of the original authorization of $1.092 billion, for Section 201, the part of the act related to the development highway system and access road program. What some researchers and journalists overlooked, even some usually careful ones, was that the authorization for Section 201 was for six years, while for all other sections of the act, it was for two years.

Despite this source of confusion and misimpression, there is no doubt that road transportation was a key part of the legislation. The possibility of obtaining highway funds provided a substantial share of the "glue" that held the PARC planning effort together. Few people familiar with much of the region would dispute that access in and through the region was below national standards and the efforts initiated in the Conference of Appalachian Governors to upgrade the road system therefore made the enterprise attractive. However, from the first efforts in 1960 onward, no one seriously involved expected that the highways by themselves would lead to a significant improvement in the regional condition. Rather, the ground transport improvements sought were viewed as a necessary but not sufficient condition for the amelioration desired. The PARC report expressed the view that "developmental activity . . . cannot proceed until the regional isolation has been overcome." The report also noted that despite the changes the completion of the interstate highway system would bring, the densely populated central part of the region would, in particular, still be ill-served. The report recommended that about half of the new Appalachian system of highways serve the people of that area, either by traversing it or cutting along its edges. In all, the highway sub-team estimated that about one person in five in the region would not be served by an interstate highway, as the interstate system and the region were then defined.

Although there is nothing in the original act which explicitly instructs the commission to construct highways according to the PARC plan and, over the years, deviations and additions have been made to it, the legislative history left no doubt that Congress was aware of the PARC recommendations and intended that they be implemented. These recommendations had resulted from the long process of investigation and negotiation of the preceding years and, as a result, the corridor locations of the basic highway system were taken as given when the legislation was enacted. With the existence of the published PARC plan, with its map and descriptions of the corridors, passage of the law turned the highways into promises that the commission felt it had to keep. Congress shared these feelings, apparently, since its latest review of the Appalachian program led to a virtual doubling of the funds authorized for Sec. 201. Since the original law was passed, the highway and access road systems have had their authorization increased three times and their mileage increased once.

Originally, the act provided for 2,350 miles of highways and 1,000 miles of local access roads at a total authorized federal cost of $840 million, with federal participation to be no more than 70% of eligible costs. In 1967, following the entry of New York into the region, the commission sought and obtained approval for a new corridor traversing the counties just north of the Pennsylvania-New York border and a connecting corridor southward to the system as previously planned. Congress approved an increase of the authorized mileage to 2,700 miles and the access road mileage authorized was increased to 1,600 miles, most of which was not intended to go to New York. At the same time, the authorized expenditure ceiling was raised to $1,015 million. In 1969, with no mileage changes involved, the authorization was raised by $150 million to $1.165 billion. Again with no further increase in authorized mileage, the latest Congressional action in 1971 has raised the funding authorization to $2.09 billion. In supporting this large increase, the commission explained that the need for extra funds to complete the system as planned arose from four sources. About 60% of the extra costs were ascribed to inflation, 20% to changes in the safety standards to which highways must be built, 10% to new requirements for assisting those displaced by federally-aided construction, and 10% to underestimates in the original preliminary engineering. It should be added that the commission's request was based on cost escalation through 1969, and that the sums now available will still be insufficient unless the states pay a larger share of the costs. Up to this point, costs have not been shared at 70:30 but rather, states have paid an average of 49% of the costs. Any further reduction in the federal share will reduce it below that now available on the regular federal aid system, i.e., 50%. That will mean that a given dollar of state funds can build more highway (by matching more federal money) off the development highway system than on it. In some states (obviously not West Virginia), this could lead to a relatively lesser emphasis on highway building in the Appalachian portion of the state.

In passing Section 201, Congress accepted the innovation of federal assistance for highways coming from general revenues, rather than from the Highway Trust Fund. It had also accepted the idea that highways could be used to induce development, rather than the traditional basis of allocating funds to highway segments that were being taxed to capacity by existing traffic. General acceptance of the recommendations of PARC meant that the commission could make implementation of the highway system an early item of business. Rapid implementation seemed desirable for a number of reasons. Some related to the long time that highway construction requires. At best, completing the system would be a long process and a delay in beginning was thought likely to delay completion. Some reasons related to the impact on Congress and the public that rapid initiation would have. This led to the "quick start" period in many programs that saw projects approved before state plans or explicit criteria were developed. Still further reasons to support prompt initiation of highway activity were the already apparent increases in construction costs. From the time of the commission's first resolutions concerning highways in May, 1965, it was clear that too little money was available to complete the system as initially conceived. In its first actions, the commission approved 87 miles of "quick start" highway projects. A map of the present development highway system is presented on page 116.

The probable shortage of funds was very much in mind as the next steps to develop more detailed plans and criteria were taken. At the same May, 1965 meeting that authorized the first highway miles, the commission defined some of the planning criteria to be followed. It established an average travel speed of 50 miles per hour between major termini as a primary objective, one that intimately affected design standards and center-line locations. It also established the goal that, to the extent possible, the highways were to be designed to standards adequate for 1990 projected traffic. And it set a norm of federal cost

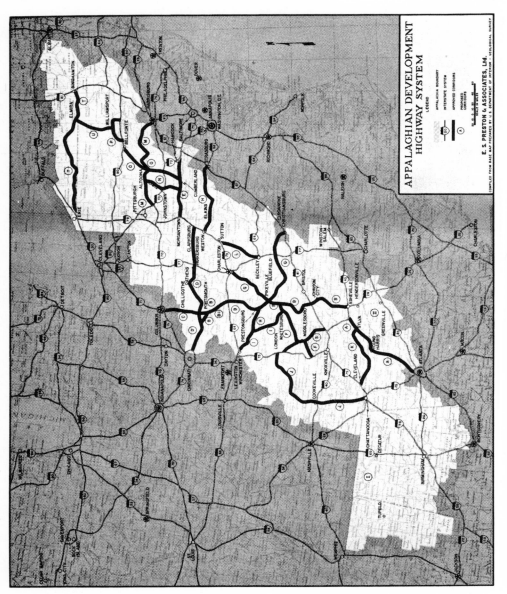

Figure 8-1. Appalachian Development Highway System.

participation at 70%. However, as noted, it was already evident that financial constraints would make that norm unattainable if extensive construction were to occur. Therefore, though the 1990 design standard was established, it was also decided to defer construction on segments adequate for 1975 projected traffic.[1] Soon the commission further defined the share of costs in which federal funds would participate. It set the standard at 70% of preliminary engineering, right-of-way acquisition and two lane construction, and at 50% of four lane construction.[2] Concern over costs was still present and another step to control them was taken in a July, 1965 resolution that established a uniform rating system under which each state would rate the adequacy of each segment of road presently in the proposed corridors.

With the information from this rating system available, it was possible to establish a more orderly procedure for highway fund distribution. Each state was given an allocation of the authorized amount[3] equal to its proportion of total miles of construction on the highway system. This set the maximum amount that each state could receive. Within that maximum, states were permitted to submit projects in priority order, beginning with those having the lowest adequacy rating, with exceptions allowed to improve route continuity or to enhance unique development opportunities. By this means, totally new segments, or those that were inadequate for existing traffic, received highest priority, followed by those likely to be strained quickly by increases in traffic. This was a rational rationing procedure within each state to the extent that the projections of traffic reflected well-grounded calculations of the traffic growth likely to occur or be induced. At that early date, and even today, it would be difficult to place high confidence levels on estimates of this type, particularly for individual segments of a 2,350 (now 2,700) mile system.

Actual construction of highways proceeded even more slowly than expected. States initially were overly optimistic about their ability to let contracts rapidly. Federal fiscal management produced "freezes" on committing highway funds which were not applied to the Appalachian system but which disrupted normal highway department procedures and morale, which did affect Appalachian events. Of crucial importance was the shortage of state funds to match the federal funds. This was most critical in West Virginia which, for all practical purposes, did not start on its share of the highway program until after 1968 when its voters approved a bond issue. On the entire system, 2,514 miles have been considered for construction, as of October 30, 1971. Of these, 572 miles are completed, 398 miles are under construction. Right-of-way is being acquired and design is underway on 944 miles more. Studies leading to location decisions are being conducted for 441 miles and no work has begun on the remaining 82 miles. In 1967, Congress extended the statutory life of Sec. 201 from June 30, 1971 to June 30, 1973. The 1971 amendments made a further extension to June 30, 1978, necessitated by the relatively slow pace of construction.

Far more commission attention, financially and in other ways, has been given to the highways authorized than to the access roads permitted by Sec. 201. Of the total funds authorized in that section, only $80 million have been allocated by the commission to the access road program. Greater emphasis on the highway program is warranted but the two are intimately related for a reason that goes beyond their authorization in the same section of the act. In its first actions concerning Sec. 201, the commission adopted the PARC corridor network which provided for no development highways in two of the original 11 states—Alabama and South Carolina. Their Appalachian areas were said to have a lesser need for major highways because of the location of the interstates in their part of the region. However, as an offset, these two states were allocated 50% of the access road mileage and funds.[4]

From the beginning, the highways were expected to have a dual purpose—to increase the economic feasibility of locating industrial activity in the region, and to increase the ability of the region's residents to commute to jobs and reach (or be reached) by public services. Over time, however, emphasis between these has tended to shift. Early decisions tended to emphasize the first of these functions. Though interstate highway standards were not sought, relatively high speed, through roads were intended. Essentially, the goal was to extend the overnight trucking distance from major centers into the region. If a state chose limited access construction, no constraints (other than financial ones) were imposed despite the fact that the commutation and service delivery functions of the highways might be lessened.

All along, but increasingly over time, the commutation and service delivery function has been emphasized. The development highway system has been likened to a giant framework on which public facilities and services are strung. In fact, it is serving that function[5] as well as the function of providing a location for industry.[6] But the two functions of a highway system would not lead to identical system designs. The industrial location function would lead to the design of high speed, limited access routes from major centers to locations of expected future economic activity. The commutation-service delivery function would lead to the design of a discontinuous system composed of spur or feeder routes from urban areas into their hinterlands, beltways around congested centers to facilitate commutation, and non-uniform design standards, some of which would be for rather low average travel speeds.

The system as actually designed is a compromise between these two types. And the method used to construct the system furthers that compromise. Political, technical and economic factors kept the commission from selecting first one corridor and then another for concentrated attention and construction.[7] Instead, as described, priority for construction has been assigned on the basis of current or imminent inadequacy. The result, until each corridor nears completion, is a series of unconnected improved segments, usually in or near larger communities. Their effect is to improve access in the locality to the services and jobs of the center. They were not consciously designed or located to bring these access improvements to those in the area. However, they do serve, at least in part, the functions that a system designed for commutation and service delivery would provide. In time, as corridors are completed, a larger element of the economic activity-inducing function may appear which would make the needs of commutation an even more compelling element in the design of additional systems. Note should be made that it is doubtful whether in the hectic climate of mid-1965 anyone connected with the program conceived that the segmented construction procedure would lead to a short-run service delivery-commutation function for the highways, gradually evolving into a longer-run, economic activity-inducing function. Hindsight has made it apparent that this is occurring.

Had clearer future vision been available, it is possible that the commission would have initially adopted a different approach to the local access road program. Despite the rather general language in Section 201 describing the functions of access roads,[8] the early emphasis was on their role as connectors to industrial parks and recreation sites—and primarily the former. Soon, greater emphasis was placed on access to educational facilities and housing sites and by 1968, the staff began to speak of access roads as "feeder roads" to the interstate or Appalachian highways from rural areas. Lately, work has been initiated on the entire range of issues involved in rural transportation systems, a reflection of the awareness that the original concept of the ground transportation system has been evolving to encompass more functions and the components they required. At the end of 1971, the commission had approved construction of 1,032 miles of the 1,600 miles authorized, consuming $66 million of the $80 million available. Four hundred ninety five miles were completed, 536 miles were under construction.

Hindsight also suggests that some highway-related activities could well have been begun earlier. Though it had supported a study of development opportunities along selected corridors,[9] only recently has the commission emphasized the use of the "borrow and fill" requirements of highways to produce level, developable sites. Also recently, it has made funds available specifically for planning concentrated investments along the highways.

In large part fortuitously, the commission's selective approach to highway construction has apparently had unforeseen benefits. It is reasonable to ask if any other benefits from the system can be discerned. Two considerations must be borne in mind as this question is examined. First, as mentioned, no one in a responsible position expected that the highways would by themselves produce a marked improvement. Secondly, only a relatively small fraction of the total construction is completed and not one corridor is finished. This makes dubious even a conventional approach to evaluation that would place major emphasis on estimates of direct economic benefits to users. Such an approach could be applied to completed segments but that would not evaluate the system. The supposition on which the system is designed is that direct user benefits are largely dependent on the completion of the system or at least, through corridors.

In an attempt to fill this analytical void, the commission has used four approaches.[10] The first takes note of the location of new industrial activity along new highways. Over 60% located within 20 minutes travel time. The inference could be drawn that prospective or actual access improvements were attractive to these firms but ARC carefully, and properly, asserts that no cause-effect relationship is known. The second approach is to find testimonial evidence concerning the highways. By and large, as can be expected, residents and officials in the affected areas would rather have access improvements than do without them and examples of benefits are cited. Third, attempts were made to calculate the increase in overnight trucking penetration into the region from major centers that will result from completion of the system. Presumably, at least some of the opportunities these calculations imply have been and will be attractive to industrial locators. Lastly, going back to a technique of the PARC highway sub-team, calculations were made of the number of people who would be beyond 25 miles of a modern highway without the development highways and with them. The number (in the 10 states receiving development highway funds) without this degree of access drops from over three million to 650,000, or 4.2% of their population. If the entire 13-state region is considered, 7.8% will not have access to a modern highway when the system is finished.

These are all potential or actual benefits, as are the commutation-service delivery benefits described earlier. However, all of them are devoid of any comparison to the costs involved and they provide no insight into the question of whether the contribution to the people of the region could have been greater if another type of expenditure had been chosen.

For the reasons previously indicated, the comparison of highway costs to benefits is not feasible now. It might be possible however to estimate that some corridors on the system are more likely to produce a better ratio of benefits to costs than others. Emphasis on these corridors at the beginning of the program might have produced larger payoffs sooner. The reality of operations made assigning priority to some corridors over others an unpromising choice to adopt, however. First, there were insufficient funds for matching federal monies and insufficient highway planning personnel in the states. Without doubt, selective emphasis on certain corridors in certain states would have delayed construction even further. Secondly, the entire implementation mechanism was designed in an environment of insufficient federal funds. It would have taken an improbable state administration to agree that funds should be concentrated in certain states first while knowing that when its state's turn arrived, the cupboard might be bare. Furthermore, delays in spending appropriated funds were a sure way to make Congress less generous when additional funds were sought.

There remains, however, the wider question of highways versus other things. This is a basic efficiency issue involving comparisons among all programs but it warrants comment here because when the question is raised, it almost invariably uses highways as an example.[11] Any answer to this question is speculative. It is hard to visualize a prosperous Appalachia without access that is significantly improved from its pre-program condition. But were the highways selected the right ones? Would better impacts have resulted from the transfer of some funds between highways and something else? Frankly, no one can say because no one has created an adequate technical basis for comparison. Technical guidance to policy decisions is therefore necessarily a blend of analysis, experience and anticipation. But policy decisions are made whether or not technical guidance is available. So estimates of effects are prepared in quantitative or qualitative terms and there is at least a presumption that decisions are no worse when that guidance is provided. Even by hindsight we will not be able to know whether a greater contribution to the well-being of the region's people would have resulted from some alternative distribution of funds. All we can know with a high degree of certainty is that in the climate of the early 1960's, without a significant highway component, there would have been no Appalachian program.

Natural Resources

A distinct evolutionary progression of ideas and policies concerning natural resources can be followed in the years since PARC's deliberations. In part, it mirrors the profound change in public attitudes towards environmental issues that have characterized this period. In part, it reflects experience and growing understanding of the natural resources component of a regional program for Appalachia.

Though there were other strands of thought present, a reading of the PARC report today makes it evident that those writing it viewed natural resources primarily as a potential contributor to regional income and output. In a sense, this was a continuation of the attitude towards natural resources that had historically characterized the region's economy. There were essentially six components to the PARC treatment and recommendations, the major ones by far being geared to resource development, as the following summary indicates.

1. Water resources—nearly $36 million, to be appropriated to existing agencies (e.g., the Farmers Home Administration, TVA and the Corps of Engineers) for the construction of water resource facilities. Ten million dollars for local water and sewer facilities.
2. Agriculture—$22 million for expanded pasture improvement programs intended to stimulate the livestock industry, which PARC felt had outstanding potential in Appalachia.
3. Timber—about $7 million to be used for expanded research in hardwood utilization; the construction of forest access roads; technical assistance for local manufacturing and marketing of Appalachian timber products; restora-

tion of depleted forest lands; and, most importantly, the creation of local timber development organizations (TDO's) that would help small land owners in development of their wood-lot holdings and processing and marketing of timber products.

4. Minerals—$3 million for research and surveys to expand utilization and markets for Appalachian minerals; continued U.S. coal export efforts; research directed towards reducing the environmental impact of mining; and specifically, research and demonstration activity related to reducing the surface subsidence caused by deep mining.
5. Power—extended studies to determine how the region might benefit from the nation's expanding power needs. No specific appropriations were recommended.
6. Recreation—No appropriations were suggested. PARC endorsed a number of pending proposals for recreation area development legislation and programs.[12]

It is noteworthy for later contrast how little of this recommended program concerned itself with environmental improvement. By the time legislation was enacted in 1965, there had been a distinct change of emphasis, whose sources can be found in pressures both within, but primarily outside, the region.

Even the legislation submitted and considered in 1964 did not fully mirror the PARC recommendations. That bill contained five sections relating directly to natural resources programs:

Sec. 203 — authorizing a pasture improvement program with a heavy emphasis on livestock production;
Sec. 204 — authorizing timber development organizations;
Sec. 205 — authorizing greater expenditures under existing mine area reclamation programs;
Sec. 206 — authorizing a water resources study to be conducted by the Army Corps of Engineers;
Sec. 212 — authorizing additional activities to provide sewage treatment facilities.

The remainder of the PARC recommendations were either omitted (for example, there was no funding of water supply facilities other than that permitted under the general supplementation section (214)) or they were left out of the proposed act and were to be handled under the existing authorizing legislation of the responsible functional agencies. [Thus, ultimately, in the first Appalachian appropriation act in 1965, $43 million was appropriated directly to agencies that were to use them to do more of their usual activities in the region. Almost all these funds were for natural resources activities, and in virtually every case, the funds were spent with little, if any, commission contribution to the expenditure decision.]

There was general, philosophical opposition to the bill in 1964 but most of the specific criticisms were directed at the various natural resources sections, producing marked changes in the proposals.

Western cattle interests actively opposed the formulation of Sec. 203. This was a period of relatively depressed domestic beef prices and further competition from what was viewed as subsidized, marginal feed lots was hardly likely to receive their encouragement. Ultimately, in 1965, the section was converted into a modification of the general soil conservation and erosion control practices program of the Department of Agriculture. As discussed in Chapter 5, timber development organizations also drew fire and the section relating to them was altered to emphasize assistance to wood-lot owners and prohibit consolidation of holdings and manufacturing, processing and marketing of wood products. Earlier, note was taken of the emasculated condition in which this left the remains of Section 204. The legislative process left Sections 206 and 212 unscathed but Section 205 was substantially altered and new, general prohibitions were added in Section 224 that forbid the use of funds under the Appalachian Act for the production, transmission or distribution of electricity or gas.

During the legislative process of 1964-65 and later, Section 205 concerning mining and mined areas underwent the greatest alteration. The PARC approach had been production oriented, with the only additional remedial program for areas of subsidence over deep mines. The supposition that additional study and research was needed before it was feasible to make recommendations of programs to overcome other effects of past mining activities was contested by several states, led by Pennsylvania. The counter-argument, which prevailed, was that existing knowledge was sufficient to begin a program to overcome these effects. The result was that the 1965 act permitted remedial steps to overcome underground mine fires and subsidence of surface lands (for which prior legislation had existed) and provided new authority to reclaim surface mined lands in public ownership. These reclamation authorities were expanded in 1967 to include the removal of waste piles resulting from underground (as well as surface) mining and from the processing of coal, and also authority to seal abandoned oil and gas wells. Further broadening of authority took place in 1971, with specific authorization to engage in projects to abate acid mine drainage pollution. The 1965 act also required that the Department of the Interior conduct a nationwide study of the effects of strip and surface mining.

In summary, by the time the initial act was signed into law, the perspective of the natural resources sections had shifted, though just barely a year had passed from the submission of the PARC report. Little was left of the emphasis on resource development as an income generator. Environmental improvement was the dominating characteristic as evidenced by the fact that by far a major share of natural resource funds appropriated in the first year ($17 million out of $28 million) was earmarked for Section 205. Though never cited as a reason for this shift, underlying it was acceptance of an economic projection. Without ever precisely saying so, policy-makers were agreeing that resource extraction would (or should) not be the important element of the regional economy that it had been. Undoubtedly strongly influential was the then continuing decline in employment in coal mining and the anticipation that mechanization of coal extraction would further diminish its importance as a regional source of employment, regardless of any reasonable upturn in the demand for coal. Only recently has the evolution of policy toward natural resources returned to a consideration of policies directly related to the economic impacts of mineral extraction.

The turn in this direction has followed the steadily broadened approach to environmental problems that characterized the first six years of program operation. In the first two years of commission operation, the staff time available for natural resources concerns was stretched thin inaugurating programs under Section 203 and 212, studying the potentials of timber development organizations and of recreation in the region, participating in the initiation of the mandated studies by the Department of the Interior and the Army Corps of Engineers, and (most time consuming of all) establishing the reclamation program authorized under Sec. 205.

Virtually all the projects approved in this period were in Pennsylvania[13] and most of them were expensive undertakings to extinguish underground mine fires and stem surface subsidence that threatened inhabited urban areas. Though in each case a relationship to the growth area emphasis of the act was established, the projects were viewed rather narrowly. Little concern was expressed about other environmental detriments in these areas and little awareness shown of the physical and economic ramifications that might follow the environmental improvement activities. A similarly narrow focus characterized the Interior Department's strip and surface mine study that was proceeding simultaneously. Though it was readily apparent that some of the surface effects of underground mining were similar to the effects of surface mining and that in some areas they were intermingled, the Interior Department study kept to the narrow focus of its authorizing statute and made no comment on the broader range of mining impacts.

Though, as noted, the commission's early program was not characterized by a very wide perspective, it was coming to recognize the inadequacy of its approach and one factor that precipitated this recognition was the need to review and comment on the Interior study. Examination of that study crystallized two negative comments, even though it was recognized that the study served the useful purpose of documenting and publicizing the extent and effects of strip and surface means of mineral extraction. The commission's negative comments focused first on the absence of any system of criteria to guide the expenditure of reclamation funds. (The commission believed it had such criteria in its growth area emphasis.) Secondly, Interior was criticized for not including the surface effects of underground mining, an aspect of the mining problem that had received considerable commission financial attention in the first two years.

The criticisms had effects in two directions. They led the president to ask that the Bureau of the Budget study the surface effects of underground mining. The resulting study supported the contention that the surface effects of underground mining were similar to those of surface extraction and that a remedial program for the environment had to include them because they were as widespread and intractable as those from more visible mining techniques. Secondly, they led the commission to seek, and obtain in the 1967 amendments, the broadened authority to reclaim waste piles and seal wells that was previously mentioned. At the same time, the request for a program to abate acid mine drainage was converted into an authorization for a study of the problem, a study that carried the evolution of policy an additional step.

During the third and fourth years of operation under Section 205, the nature of approved projects changed. The principal projects designed to overcome threats to urban areas in Pennsylvania had been approved and now the emphasis shifted to surface reclamation to create areas suitable for development or recreation use. A broader perspective was applied. It not only asked what the problems from prior mining were and where they were, it also asked more inquiringly about the uses to which reclaimed areas were to be put. In the first two years, when inhabited areas were threatened, the last category of question was considered largely extraneous. Now its pertinence was clearer and before projects were approved, alternatives and the associated activities needed to capitalize on the reclamation were more specifically examined. In brief, emphasis shifted from overcoming threats to improving prospects, from first-aid to a recuperative concern for the effects of extraction on the region's future.

Simultaneous with this shift, the acid mine drainage study proceeded, seeking to assess the need, desirability and conditions under which public and private remedial programs might be warranted and the nature of them. Two general conclusions stemmed from the study. First, it was found that there had probably been considerable overstatement of the deleterious economic effects of acid mine drainage on the region. Secondly, the most serious measurable effects were on the supply of recreation opportunities in parts of the region but that in these areas, other environmental problems were also degrading their recreation potential. Combined, these conclusions suggested that controlling acid mine drainage should be part of a more general pollution control effort and that priority should be assigned to areas with water and water-related needs that could not be satisfied at lesser cost by other means. More broadly, the study widened perspectives still further. It made clear the need to view the environmental impacts of mining as part of the environmental system of an area. It highlighted the desirability of an approach to environmental improvement that encompassed the entire range of environmental impacts impinging on the area. The commission therefore recommended that Congress add an environmental evaluation to the list of factors it must consider before projects can be approved. The first Senate version of the 1971 extension included this and though not included in the amended act, it will probably become a self-imposed requirement. The commission will have moved from a project-by-project approach to mine reclamation to an environmental improvement approach that recognizes the interaction of complementary investments to further the development of areas.

In pace with the heightened demand for coal and the public concern about the effects of mining on miners and the environment, the commission's program has taken another turn. Returning to the theme of resource extraction, the commission now has conducted studies of the demand for coal and coal manpower, the role that mineral taxation can play in state and local finance, coal manpower training, and the responsibilities of the states under mine safety and mining control laws. In a sense, this is a return to an emphasis on natural resource extraction as an industry but the return is with a broader perspective on the effects of mining on people and on the region. Evidence of ARC's continued involvement in environmental enhancement can be found in its support and participation in a program to remove environmental deterrents to development in the Monongehela River Basin.

In the commission's operations, it is artificial to separate program operation from policy evolution. Those who administer programs, recommend policies, and insights gained in administering one program are translated into the operation and policies of others. Yet program operation is a conceptually separable aspect. Earlier, in Chapter 6, operations under Sections 204 and 205 were discussed. Here, the programs authorized by Sections 203, 205 and 212 will be summarized.

Section 203

Though modeled after the regular Agricultural Conservation Program (ACP) of the Department of Agriculture, the program included in the Appalachian Act differs from it in two principal respects. The regular ACP operates on a year-to-year basis, requiring individual contracts with farmers for each year. The farmers have no assurance that continuing support will be available for a long-term program of improvement. Under Section 203, three to ten year contracts were permitted to be made with landowners, operators or occupiers of land for land stabilization, erosion and sediment control, reclamation through changes in land uses, and the establishment of conservation and development measures. Secondly, the regular ACP contracts provide for a 50% cost sharing by the federal government. Section 203 raised the federal percentage to 80%, allowing larger numbers of poorer farmers to participate.

The day-to-day operation of this program is conducted through the local committees, supervised by the Department of Agriculture, that administer the regular ACP activities. ARC participation principally concerned two aspects—the selection of the list of approved practices which might be included in the contracts and the geographic areas within the region eligible for participation. This latter attempt at concentration was perhaps the most novel aspect of the program since it stands in such contrast with the traditional approach in ACP, which is to obtain the widest possible dispersion of the available funds.

The commission required that each state produce a plan for the use of Section 203 funds that was consistent with and related to its plan for the overall development of its portion of the region. The areas selected for Section 203 expenditures had to be either growth areas designated by the state or the state had to show how investments outside these areas will serve them, for example, by reducing siltation that affects the water resources of the growth area.

At the time the program was enacted, it was estimated that 8.6 million acres in the region needed the kinds of treatment that Section 203 allows. Of course, not all these acres qualified under the restrictive geographic conditions imposed by the commission. Fund limitations and other priorities make it doubtful that any such mass improvement program would even be warranted. However, in the first six years of operation, almost $16.7 million of federal funds was involved in about 15,700 contracts. Over 400,000 acres were involved.

Obtaining concentrated investments was not easy since the established ACP mechanisms find virtue in wide distribution but with each fiscal year, a trend toward concentration in fewer and fewer areas was evident. In the first year of the program, more than one-third of the counties then in the region were listed as eligible in the state plans. By fiscal 1970, the number of eligible areas had fallen to about one-sixth the regional total. Evidence that concentration has occurred can also be seen in the comparison of the average size of contracts under Section 203 and ACP. These exceed $1,000 while under the regular ACP, they do not average $200.

Commission support for this program has ended. No new appropriations were obtained in the last two years and the last date for instituting new contracts with farmers or amending old ones was November 30, 1971. From the time that the program was altered following the congressional debate of 1964, there was never much enthusiasm for the program because no one was convinced that it was well designed or of sufficient magnitude to address a serious problem. It can be documented that operations on over 200,000 acres have been completed, that over 250,000 acres of pasture have been improved, that over 13,000 acres have benefited from channel improvements and surface water erosion control, and so on. What cannot be asserted in a measurable way is that the program has had favorable impacts beyond the fences of the farms involved. Such effects would mostly be indirect and be obscured by the welter of other influences at work. Moreover, the range of on-farm benefits was probably limited by the legislative requirement that contracts with each individual be limited to no more than 50 acres of treatment. Even if a farmer had the resources to participate in a more extensive program, the law precluded such an agreement.

Section 205

The briefest examination of the legacy that coal mining has left in Appalachia makes it apparent why great selectivity was needed in allocating the limited funds available under Section 205 for mine area reclamation. In 1965, over 10,000 miles of stream in the region were polluted from mining operations, over 515,000 acres had been stripped and not reclaimed, in an average year two to three cases of surface subsidence in inhabited areas occurred, and more than 27 major underground mine fires in or around urban areas existed in Pennsylvania which also had close to 300 burning surface waste piles, all releasing toxic fumes.

A basis for selection was immediately apparent in some cases, however. Fires beneath cities and subsidence of urban, inhabited property were granted higher priority for remedial action than situations not endangering health and safety. Acres disturbed by surface mining that were remote from urban areas and unlikely to be developed could be given a far lower priority than the roughly 35,000 acres that were more probably developable. Similarly, burning waste piles that were far from inhabited areas did not pose a priority environmental problem. However, further selectivity was required in the use of the available funds.

Section 205 set two additional limits. Federal funds could provide no more than 75% of the cost of reclamation. Strip mine reclamation had to be on public lands to forestall windfall gains to private landowners. Additionally, the growth area prescription of the act applies to this section. In practice, all these limitations combined to produce a restricted list of available projects, most of them in Pennsylvania. The bulk of the available funds (over $29 million) have been spent there.

Through December 31, 1971, 52 projects had been approved. The annual expenditures exceed $2 million. Twenty six projects were for extinguishing mine fires, 15 to control subsidence, 9 to restore surface areas and two to cap wells. Individual projects have been useful in protecting life and property and in creating and preserving opportunities. For example, an industrial park threatened by a mine fire was protected. Elsewhere, a major state recreation investment was enhanced and a site for a school created. Overall, the investment has not been large and though cost-benefit analysis was not applied to the individual projects, they could probably have been justified on a strict efficiency basis.

Administration of this program has not been simple. Major responsibilities were assumed by the Bureau of Mines and by the state mining agencies. In many cases, their internal mechanisms operated to delay the steps necessary to get work underway so that it is not unusual to find no work begun a year or two (and sometimes three) after a project had been approved. In this area, as in others, a price was paid for the decision to keep the commission staff small and to avoid duplicating the technical competency of existing federal and state agencies.

Section 212

The Commission established rather rigid requirements for approval of projects under Section 212 because it recognized that the potential demand for waste treatment funds was virtually unlimited. This was true even before the recent heightened emphasis on environmental matters and was certainly true after it. Consequently, the commission required that projects under this section show direct and demonstrable impact on the economic growth of an area designated for investment concentration in a state plan. Strict adherence to this point of view, which essentially limits waste water treatment to cases where it can serve as a necessary condition of economic growth, has been difficult to enforce. About 30% of the available funds were not so concentrated because of the persuasiveness of the counter-view that sewage treatment is a requirement for health and should be made available broadly. As of the end of 1971, ARC had spent over $32 million on sewage treatment system. Of this, $5.4 million was appropriated under Section 212 and the balance ($27 million) under Section 214.

With the greater availability of funds under regular federal programs, no new appropriations for Section 212 have been sought or received in the last three fiscal years but the policy issue of the desirable degree of concentration remains because it also affects the use of Section 214 funds to supplement the regular federal programs. Recently, the commission has been actively (and sometimes heatedly) reviewing its policies, pressed by applications supported by some states for investments in areas quite remote from designated growth areas but with acknowledged problems in meeting water quality standards. Though centering on a relatively narrow investment question, at its root is the issue of whether or not there can be working separation between a program designed to implement a development strategy and one concerned with welfare in an immediate and general sense.

Equally troublesome has been ARC's inability to prod the federal government into a coherent program of sewage treatment grants. Neither the states nor ARC have prevented various federal agencies, particularly the Environmental Protection Agency and Farmers Home Administration, from making grants on such narrow geographic bases that the goal of a basin or sub-region treatment system is stymied. A grant to one unit of government within the area precludes its participation in a geographically broader program but the economic and physical requirements of a feasible broader system may require that governmental unit's participation.

Education Activities

When ARC began to direct concerned attention to the educational problems of the region, it found a situation which can be summarized as containing the following elements:

1. An assessment from the PARC report that the region suffered from a significant educational achievement lag when national standards were applied.
2. A prior anticipation of concerted activities with OEO to remedy some of these deficiencies that was already showing signs of the division to come.
3. A law that provided special assistance for the construction of vocational education facilities (Sec. 211) and supplementation of other education construction and equipment programs (through the use of Sec. 214 funds), primarily the equipment title (IV) of the Elementary and Secondary School Act, the Higher Education Facilities Act and the Library Services Act.
4. Legislation that provided no assistance in meeting the operating costs of education and no stated responsibility for curriculum matters or other dimensions of educational quality.[14]
5. A growing awareness of a human resources development versus economic growth dilemma that its policies had to resolve. For example, the language of Section 211, concerning vocational education facilities, speaks of "grants ... in areas ... in which such education is not now adequately available" without specific recognition of the mandate in Section 2 of the act to concentrate investments "in areas where there is a significant potential for future growth."

This situation, combined with an increasing flow of project applications, led the commission to take two steps. The first was to establish the guidelines for the use of its appropriated monies for education projects that were discussed in Chapter 5. In essence, they state a preference for investments in growth areas but do not preclude educational investments elsewhere. Secondly, it established an Education Advisory Committee composed of one representative from each state plus an equal number of federal co-chairman appointees. This group was asked to evaluate the region's educational system, to recommend improved methods of using the powers conferred by Sections 211 and 214, and to propose new programs and procedures for possible implementation at all levels of government. Gradually, an education staff was created, first directly responsible to the committee and then as an element of the commission staff. The ARC policies that have evolved have largely been initiated by the committee and the associated staff and its consultants.

The Education Advisory Committee members from the states tended to come from the state education departments and, in practice, they operated with little direct supervision from, and sometimes without the knowledge of, their governor's representative to the commission. The effect of this separation was to lead to some uncertainty about the authority with which these committee members spoke. It was never perfectly clear whether the position of a state member of the committee was also that of his state's administration. In his home state, he tended to have only that influence over state education policy and related state agencies which his regular position bestowed upon him. Frequently, this meant that little power could be found among the state appointees. Much the same could be said about the federal appointees who represented diverse interests and experiences but not the Department of Health, Education and Welfare or the Office of Education. In practice, it was these organizations whose policies and programs were needed to improve regional educational conditions. The opportunity to commit them to regional goals was missed by not having their responsible representatives participate in the committee's activities. Overall, a different composition of the committee might have made it a more useful device, even though, with its existing composition, it has proved useful.

The committee's recommendations have been made in a series of reports, the first of which, in January 1968, provided an overview of the deficiencies in Appalachian education. Data showed the region lagged behind the nation in financial support, qualified manpower, quality of facilities and programs, pupil retention, and services to students. Resources were deemed unlikely to be available to create remedial activities in all these areas and the committee recommended concentration on:

1. State long-range, comprehensive education planning,
2. Construction and operation of vocational schools,
3. Revision of elementary and junior high school regular courses to increase their relevancy to the "world of work,"
4. Establishment of education programs for children three through eight,
5. Encouragement of training of teachers and teacher aides,
6. Encouragement of the creation of regional education cooperative organizations as a way to overcome the adverse financial effects of inefficiently small school districts and inadequate financial bases.

Several aspects of these recommendations are noteworthy. First, and perhaps most surprising, no mention was made of the need for a more far-reaching improvement in primary and secondary education than merely to increase their relevancy to employment.[15] Secondly, and closely related to this, there is no specific mention of the need for state-local joint efforts. Despite this omission, in six states, the state member of the committee was eventually able to have created a state-wide advisory committee which he chaired. His policy positions on the committee then began to reflect a local, as well as state, point of view. Third, the special emphasis on vocational education and the modest mention of higher education reflect a system of priorities that others have questioned. For example, it has been contended that the vocational education emphasis is designed to perpetuate a "colonial" status for Appalachia in its relations with the rest of the country and particularly its major, extra-regional employers.

The commission responded to the committee's recommendations by adopting them as its education priorities. It has continued to be responsive to committee recommendations, including the change in emphasis that led to the present research activities that inquire about opportunities for higher education that exist for the Region's youth. This responsiveness has resulted in a restatement of priorities. In its 1970 annual report, the commission said:[16]

On advice from its Educational Advisory Committee, the Commission adopted six general priorities for dealing with educational problems in Appalachia:

1. Develop job-relevant technical and vocational training opportunities.
2. Form multi-jurisdictional educational cooperatives to help facilitate the area-sharing of school services by initiating a selected number of such cooperative arrangements in various parts of the region.
3. Within the framework of the local educational cooperatives, upgrade the quantity and quality of teachers in Appalachia.
4. Also within the cooperatives, promote the development of early childhood education.
5. Provide improved occupational information and guidance.
6. Promote comprehensive state planning for educational improvement.

The Commission subsequently adopted a seventh priority: to develop new approaches to the training of manpower from rural areas.

In March 1971, the committee submitted 48 recommendations to the commission.[17] They are designed to help achieve these goals but it is too soon to gauge the influence they will have.

An almost classic example of the impact of a research report is the response to a December, 1968 committee presentation analyzing the vocational education system of the region.[18] In brief, the report documented a gross mis-match between evolving job demands and the existing program emphases in the region's secondary school vocational education programs. The presentation of this report was followed by an amendment to the commission's criteria for granting assistance in the construction of vocational education facilities. The applicant has to demonstrate that the training courses to be offered are related to existing or projected demands for manpower in the sub-region or the nation. Using its power over funds appropriated for construction, the commission exercised an effective influence over curriculum content and forced a broadening of perspective beyond the local labor market. Implied was a tacit acknowledgment that out-migration might be in the interest of some of the region's younger citizens. In this almost unheralded way, the commission responded to two of the perplexing issues it faced. Though it was given no direct authority to influence educational quality, it made its priorities felt in at least one area and it took a position on the potentially explosive issue of out-migration. It took this means to give some content to its goal of better equipped citizens "wherever they may choose to live."

Through the end of 1971, $106 million of commission funds have been invested in vocational education facilities. These funds assisted 260 facilities that provide both secondary and post-secondary education opportunities, as well as retraining programs and upgrading opportunities for adults. More than half the facilities supported are now open for use and they are beginning to have their impact on the education experience available. In fiscal 1966, only 38% of the enrollments in secondary school vocational education were in programs leading to 95% of the jobs projected to be available in 1975. By fiscal 1969, this figure had risen to 44%.

Overall, commission supported facilities have added more than 125,000 day time student spaces to the educational plant of the region (plus places for an unknown number of night and weekend students). This is about one-fourth of the total increase in capacity that has occurred in the nation in the years of ARC activity. During these years, regional secondary school attendance rose 13%, while vocational enrollments rose 34%. Since the start of commission activity, secondary school vocational education enrollments rose two and a half times faster than in the nation as a whole. The same relative rate of increase has existed in the adult, post-high school groups. In fact, criticism can be directed toward this program because of its tendency to underestimate the demand for spaces and consequently to underbuild.

Various states have devised different patterns for satisfying the demand for this kind of education but some are of particular interest. Kentucky, with a rather unique problem of a dispersed student population, has developed a system of satellite education centers at which some aspects of vocational training can be offered before students are transported longer distances to take advantage of more expensive facilities at an area-serving school. South Carolina has developed a program of paramedical education that is a national model. A similar description can be given to the residential program Ohio created at Nelsonville and the program for training for the recreation industry offered at Asheville, North Carolina. Virginia used the availability of funds under the Appalachian Act to complete a network of post-secondary technical institutes through its part of the region.

These institutes, part of a community college system, are, in a sense, a bridge between secondary and traditional higher education. The commission has supported a wider range of higher education activities than originally recommended by its advisory committee. It has supported activities in teacher and teacher aide training (as recommended) but it has also made investments using Section 214 funds, in a rather wide range of institutions (85) for a larger number of facilities (135). Higher education institutions in every state have received support, sometimes assisting the creation of what is, in essence, a new "education growth center" such as in Cookeville, Tennessee. In other cases, main campus facilities for the dominant state institutions have received support. Overall, the commission spent $46 million supplementing the Higher Education Facilities Act through 1971.

In the years since the first recommendations of the advisory committee were made, far more understanding has been gained by all concerned of the necessary content of the regional cooperative agencies suggested. As now understood, they may become the vehicle for implementing some of the other recommendations for improved education services. The long range planning assistance provided to the states has tended to focus first on this aspect of institution-building. What have come to be called Regional Education Service Agencies (RESA) are arrangements between school districts to provide jointly and to share services that would be uneconomic for each to provide alone. The concept is not new and, in fact, mandatory or permissive legislation exists in some Appalachian states. Though there are legal and technical issues involved, a major problem is the tradition of separateness, of independence, that helps explain the perpetuation of the inefficient school districts in the first place. The commission effort has therefore been directed toward creating nearby model RESA's so that neighboring districts can witness their operations and see if advantages exist for them. This effort is relatively recent and thus far less than $2 million in planning grants have been made by ARC. The commission has made 15 of these grants to groups that are planning, for example, for in-service training, teaching aides, programs for early childhood and youth, curriculum revision, and school drop-out identification and counseling. The progress made led Congress to amend the act in 1971 to permit funds appropriated under Section 211 to be used to support the demonstration program operations of RESA's.

An even more noteworthy and potentially far-reaching amendment to Section 211 was passed in 1971. It permits grants to cover operating deficits of ongoing vocational education programs. This is a relatively novel provision and commission policy to guide its implementation is still being decided. However, the use of the new authority will probably be limited to multi-district projects that use public facilities and provide means for evaluating their programs of areawide educational planning, services and programs for students.

Gradually, an unique role has emerged for the education staff that has proven to yield a relatively important product. The staff has become a broker for the educational interests of the region, helping to increase the availability of federal funds to the region and the ability of local groups to take advantage of their availability. It is impossible to establish the exact magnitude of the staff's effects but the impact of its research in areas such as education manpower quality and availability,[19] for example, may partly explain the doubling of the allocation of funds to the region under the Education Professions Development Act between fiscal 1969 and 1970. In other cases, by working with the Office of Education during the preparation of program guidelines, it has been possible to make certain that decisions were made in full cognizance of their implications for the region—and to its benefit.

Working at the problem from the other end, the education staff has held seminars to assist Appalachian districts and other institutions in the preparation of grant requests, while continuing to press on the Office of Education the need for the projects requested. A dollar value cannot be put on the projects whose acceptance was assisted, nor can the effects of the projects be measured. All available evidence suggests, however, that the region has been advantaged by the ambassadorial role performed.

The character and quality of the educational investments and activities of the commission may prove to be among its more important ones. Certainly, they will profoundly affect the training opportunities available to several million students in the years to come. Another aspect of this experience is important too, however. The conversion of a program initially restricted to facilities to one concerned with services and their delivery is noteworthy. A change in emphasis from building buildings to helping create regional service agencies, revise curricula and increase the availability and quality of educational manpower is indicative of an important lesson to be learned from this experience. The concept of the education role of the commission embodied in the original act was insufficient. No program that attempts to use education as a contributant to regional development can successfully narrow its concerns to a small element of the education process. And no program of regional development is likely to be successful without an education component.[20]

Measured strictly in dollar terms, the commission made the following commitments to education by the end of 1971:

Academic Education	$	483,459
Educational TV		2,295,156
Higher Education Facilities		45,918,951
Libraries		7,010,664
National Defense Education Grant Supplements		5,537,171
Vocational Education		106,541,434.

Youth Leadership

A small, relatively recent, and relatively unremarked component of the Appalachian effort is a program in youth leadership. Its existence is a reflection of the commission's attempts to broaden the scope of its activities to encompass more aspects of the region's problems and potentials. One major stimulus of the activities underway was the emphasis on youth during the legislative authorization hearings in 1969. The timing of the program's initiation is evidence that it is part of a more general, national response to the so-called "youth revolution." However, the problem to which it is addressed is also rooted in the region's demographic and political structure.

The demographic aspects of the situation are those common to any area of relative distress. Its highly mobile young population, particularly those with comparatively better educations and between 18 and 34, leave the region. In addition to the obvious personal aspects of such a tendency, there is also a high economic cost to this mobility because of the embodied educational investment in those who migrate. (Estimates are that at least half of the region's outmigrants are in this age group.) And there is a high social cost in the loss of leadership potential for the region that the outmigrants could have supplied.

Whether a cause or effect of the region's distress (and perhaps both), the local political structure in much of the region has tended to be conservative and self-perpetuating, producing in the minds of many residents a belief that pressure for desired changes through the established political instruments was likely to be unproductive. These attitudes, transmitted to the young people of the region, were believed to inhibit their inclinations to become involved in the region's problems and, perhaps, contributed to their tendency to outmigrate.

In a sense, the entire ARC effort can be viewed as an attempt to relieve the root cause of this migration by broadening the range of opportunities available within the region. However, the youth leadership program is a small attempt to get directly at the economic, social and political aspects of the youth problem. It is designed to provide experiences that may persuade the youth of the region that they can potentially do something about its problems and that therefore there might be a future for them in the region.

In more formal terms, the program was established:[21]

To assess the nature of the impending crisis in leadership in Appalachia, statistically define the problem, and help the states and development districts create public awareness of the need for more young people to become educated and trained as future leaders of the region.

To enlist the public and private institutions of the region, particularly the schools, to more effectively meet their responsibilities in the development of new leadership.

To work with various service and voluntary associations to promote more active participation by talented citizens in developing the region. Also, to work with businesses and other groups to stimulate youth employment.

To create among the young people in the region a pride in its past, an awareness of Appalachia's considerable future potential, an understanding of its problems, and a commitment to stay in the region and help build a better future.

The goal of the project is to assist the student in realizing that he can cause things to happen rather than have them happen to him. The project also gives the student an opportunity to see how today's leaders fulfill their leadership roles.

To achieve objectives as sweeping as these far more funds than the approximately $300,000 per fiscal year expended by the commission would be required, even if the techniques for achieving them were better understood. However, they are not and this, among other reasons, counseled a modest series of exploratory undertakings. Thus far, the activities conducted have originated in applications from LDD's, states, or individual institutions whose planning for this program was assisted by the very small commission staff devoted to the enterprise.

Projects receiving support have included the financing of hundreds of summer interns in LDD's and other public agencies. In one LDD, a youth council was established which is seeking to develop a recreation park and a child development program. In one state, a program designed to provide short-term assistants to public agencies was devised. Its structure was intended to lead to better understanding between higher education and other institutions of the state and to make students aware of the public service opportunities available to them. Other districts have focused on establishing youth councils on social awareness, sponsoring seminars and internships in agencies dealing with programs like model cities, all designed to lead to wider involvement in social and economic development. One district is trying simulation techniques to develop motivation while another is engaged in an entrepreneurial development program. In one state, a program to foster knowledge and respect for the history and culture of the mountainous area is underway. Programs to assist returning job corpsmen and "high risk" college students are underway. Thus far, several thousand young people have been involved.

The range of activities is quite broad and could potentially be broader.[22] The recent (1969) initiation of the program makes it more than unlikely that observable impacts have yet occurred. In the nature of this type of enterprise, effects will be difficult to identify and, as a result, careful monitoring and evaluative follow-ups are important because this is a field in which much more needs to be known. At this point, however, note can be taken of this program as a rather novel component of an approach to regional development and of the commission's awareness of its importance. In its *1970 Annual Report*[23] it asserts, "The program attempts to deal with a basic and troubling concern which questions the entire future of the region. If the youth of Appalachia cannot be convinced that there is hope in the region and that there are constructive outlets for their meaningful involvement in solving its problems, then all the other programs, no matter how ably administered or how wisely planned, will ultimately fail."

Housing

In any national, competitive search for wretched housing, there is a good chance that Appalachia would win. There are some rural areas whose housing is substandard in 90% of the cases and overall, the latest data suggest that over 1 million of the region's dwelling units need substantial repair or replacement.

Facts like these were well-known in 1964. The PARC report makes note of them and then points to credit unavailability as a major reason for the problem. No legislative follow-up occurred, however, because the revisions in national housing legislation then gestating were expected to relieve the problem.

This proved to be an unwarranted anticipation. In its first two years of operation, and particularly as credit tightened in 1966, the commission found itself without a program but with growing concerns in the housing field. Some state plans identified housing inadequacies as important social and health problems and also pointed to the condition of existing housing as an inhibitor of economic growth. Other states, in reviewing the situation, pointed to the potential direct economic impact from greater housing construction activity. Other agencies (HUD and OEO, as well as state and state-supported institutions) asked for comments on programs to stimulate home repair and the design of new types of units.

Throughout this period, and largely on the initiative of one staff member, the elements of a policy position began to emerge. As later study supported, in addition to the national factors that lead to constraints on housing production for low and moderate income families, there were additional ones in Appalachia. These are relatively higher construction costs coupled with a shortage of developable sites in parts of the region, the failure of governments and other groups to be aware of and take advantage of existing programs, and inadequate professional services to finance and "package" housing projects so that they could receive support from existing programs. This latter factor, the relative unavailability of risk capital as "front" money for the planning of projects and the shortage of talent to conceive, execute and manage housing projects was particularly prevalent.

This led to a proposal to the commission, and from it to Congress, which became the basis for Section 207 of the act, which was added in 1967. It creates an Appalachian Housing Fund to provide planning grants and also loans of up to 80% of the "front" money not otherwise available to purchase the services required. The fund is reimbursed for its advances from the mortgages obtained by the housing sponsors.

The commission views its housing program as having a two-fold purpose:

1. To create more sponsors for low and moderate income housing projects,
2. To provide technical assistance to states, localities, and private sponsors in launching major housing programs in the region.

When originally establishing procedures to implement the new section, the commission required that the projects be in areas of significant potential for future growth, since the law contained this stipulation. This limitation was removed in the 1971 amendments which permits ARC to establish eligible areas. It has not deviated from its former decision on area eligibility. Also in 1971, the authority of Section 207 was expanded to permit financial assistance to cover site-development costs, a move designed to help expand the supply of available sites.

Commission activities in the housing field have fallen into two general categories—financial assistance and technical assistance. In the financial area, by the end of 1971 loans of about $2.8 million had been approved on projects designed to produce almost 7,700 units at a total cost of about $98 million. (For comparative purposes, it should be noted that from the beginning of the federal housing programs in 1961 through 1967, they had led to the construction of 602 units in Appalachia.) Over one-third of the housing units supported under Section 207 are occupied.

Technical assistance activities have led to the creation of state housing programs. Beginning with Kentucky and West Virginia, but later including North Carolina, state housing corporations have been established by law. The commission has provided financial and other assistance for their initial organizing activities. These corporations are designed to implement state housing policy and to overcome the shortage of funds by issuing their own tax-exempt instruments. They use the proceeds to buy federally insured mortgages and construction loans. Their ability to commit funds in advance for these purposes substantially overcomes the financial hurdles for sponsors of low- and moderate-income housing. Less sweeping programs have been developed for Maryland, Ohio, Pennsylvania and South Carolina and advice and assistance have been made available to numerous localities, organizations and individuals.

Several comments are warranted by this experience. First, as the preceding chapter suggested, this is an example of programmatic entrepreneurship that ideally should characterize a wider range of commission activities and that (perhaps) would be more common had the staff been larger. Secondly, the data show that Section 207 has been able to stimulate greater construction activity in the region and, in fact, has been cited as a model by the Advisory Commission on Intergovernmental Relations. Moreover, the idea of Section 207 has now been made available nationally through Section 106 of the National Housing Act of 1968.

All this is to the credit of the Appalachian effort. A fundamental offset to this optimistic view is the continued deplorable shape of the housing of millions of the region's citizens, most notably in Central Appalachia. Section 207 and the activities following its enactment were imaginative and useful but far more construction will need sponsorship before a discernible impact on the housing situation can be observed. That is why the technical assistance program of the commission will ultimately be more important than the number of housing projects it directly supports. Stimulation of states and LDD's to recognize the need for a housing policy and program and support of their efforts to develop plans and organizations to achieve their goals helps create the continuing base from which a more profound impact on the supply of housing may be made.

Health Care and Early Childhood Programs[24]

Implementation of the demonstration health program authorized by Section 202 of the act is virtually a case study of the travails of attempted innovation. From the time of its first mention in the PARC report, this component of the Appalachian program was grounded on the belief that pioneering was required even to provide Appalachians with the level of health care available, on the average, to the people of the country. It was also hoped that this effort would emphasize preventive care and might point to options available to the nation as a whole in upgrading the delivery of health care.

PARC recommended the creation of several multipurpose regional health centers that could each serve as a single, major source of health services. By the time the Appalachian Act was before the Congress, the form of the concept had shifted to supporting the construction of multicounty demonstration health facilities, such as "hospitals, regional health diagnostic and treatment centers, and other facilities necessary for health" and included authorization for the use of federal funds to pay a gradually declining share of the operating deficits of the facilities constructed for their first five years. The entire concept, and particularly the payment of operating deficits, was expected to draw heavy opposition from the health care delivery associations which were in the midst of their vain attempts to defeat the Medicare proposals then before Congress. Perhaps because their attention was diverted by the major battle they were fighting, no opposition of any moment to the provisions of Section 202 appeared and without fanfare, for the first time Congress approved the use of federal funds to cover some of the operating costs of non-federal health facilities.

Recognizing that it had a novel program to administer, the commission sought guidance from a Health Advisory Committee that it established in October, 1965. The result of this committee's activities was a total rethinking of the concept of the program, with attendant delays in implementation since, in part, amendment of the law was required. It was not until August, 1968 that funding of projects under this section actually began.

The committee made two signal recommendations. In the first, they urged the use of local groups to direct the demonstration program in their areas and in the second, they argued for a shift in program emphasis away from facilities. It was this latter recommendation that required Congressional assent. The committee argued that Appalachia's principal health care problem was not a shortage of buildings, but of services. They therefore recommended that Section 202 funds be used to trigger a series of experimental service delivery programs, that Section 214 funds be used to aid in the construction of any additional facilities, and that the law allow Section 202 funds to be used to cover operating deficits of existing and new facilities that were not built with 202 funds. They urged that the law also permit reimbursement for operating deficits of programs that did not require facilities, such as home nursing programs.

The commission accepted the committee's recommendations in January, 1966 but full implementation required the Congressional assent that was not received until the 1967 amendments were adopted. Under Section 202 as amended, the Secretary of Health, Education and Welfare was authorized to make three types of grants after approval by the Appalachian Regional Commission: planning grants of up to 75 percent of total cost; construction and equipment grants of up to 80 percent; and grants to cover up to 100 percent of operating deficits for the first two years of a project, and up to 75 percent of such costs for the following three years.

Within one year of its creation, the commission had recommended a change that was in keeping with the general evolution of its emphases. It was moving toward the conversion of what had been thought of as a facilities-oriented program to one that also emphasized service delivery.

Before Congressional assent for the change in focus was received, the process of selecting areas for the demonstrations was begun, utilizing state personnel, a very few ARC staff members and a small number of people lent by the Public Health Service. The advisory committee had recommended that the areas generally conform to health service areas and that they also give evidence of readiness to engage in this novel demonstration. One evidence of this readiness was the ability to constitute a broadly based group that included representatives of both providers and consumers of health care. In some areas, local health care personnel viewed the possibility of a demonstration program as part of a scheme to revamp the private practice of medicine. To assuage these fears, the commission amended its guidelines to state that the programs under Section 202 "shall preserve and encourage all existing programs and arrangements involving the relationship between the physician and the patient." This language is so vague that it would not necessarily preclude innovation and there is no clear evidence that it has done so. However, the fact that it was needed to secure cooperation is indicative of an attitude that probably has inhibited innovation in the program. Other, more specific inhibitions to innovation have existed however.

On the basis of judgment about community readiness, and in accord with its expressed desire to fund demonstrations in a variety of areas within the region, the commission has established 12 health demonstration areas, seven in 1967, one each in 1968 and 1969 and the rest in 1970. Significant programs have not begun in those three areas established recently.

One of the areas crosses the state boundary between Georgia and Tennessee and all the Appalachian states have a health demonstration area except New York, which has now been allocated funds to institute one. In all, the 12 areas now designated include 110 of the 397 Appalachian counties plus, for planning purposes only, 3 non-Appalachian counties (one in North Carolina and two in Mississippi). Overall, these areas include some of the counties with the worst health statistics in the region, though the area averages are about the same as those for the region as a whole.

The local boards initiate the program elements to be operated in their areas and therefore the composition of the boards is a key to understanding the experience with program operation. By and large, members of the local boards come from the same community groups whose members serve on local development district boards. They are the civic leaders, whether elected or not. They serve on the boards of community organizations, particularly those which are health-related; they serve with other social service groups, such as education; they represent the health care delivery professions and particularly the physicians. Despite these similarities, the degree of dominance by health professionals differs among the boards and the impression among those associated with the program is that the less the dominance of the health care professionals, the more variety of program suggestions considered.

Before actual designation as a demonstration occurred, each area prepared a plan that detailed the health care availability and health needs and problems in its area. It then recommended the steps which it felt should be taken. These plans, which distill the judgments of the locality as represented on the board, have until recently been updated annually. The procedure now is to require a four-year plan with an annual updating and a statement of intended activities during the year. The change is symptomatic of a basic problem. Initially, the plans did not establish a firm relationship between the needs and problems of an area and the recommended program. Annual plans were required in anticipation that in succeeding years, a better "fit" would be obtained but this has not occurred to any marked degree. In part, the explanation for this lies within the commission staff structure which has always devoted too few professionally trained people to the task of reviewing the area plans and working with the boards to improve the relationship between their analysis and their recommended actions.

Examination of the projects and programs funded under Section 202 provides some insight into the extent to which the intended emphasis has actually occurred. In fiscal 1970, for example, $14.1 million of Section 202 funds were authorized for planning and operating programs and $26.2 million for construction. From the first grant through fiscal 1970, about 58% of the Section 202 funds were authorized for construction purposes. The financial overbalance in favor of construction would seem to conflict with the recommendation of the Health Advisory Committee. This may well be the case, for reasons soon to be evident, but the financial data alone cannot be interpreted in this way with certainty. Capital costs will always bulk large in the beginning phases of a program such as this and the program is quite young. Moreover, some areas do not conform to the general pattern in their need for facilities or in their relative emphasis between planning and operation and construction. In the same year, fiscal 1970, the Alabama area received $2.6 million for planning and operations and $1.8 million for construction, North Carolina $1.4 million versus 1.1 million, and the West Virginia area was authorized $2.4 million for planning and operations and $.2 million for construction.

Cumulative expenditures under Section 202 through January 1, 1972 give one indication of the overall magnitude of the commission's efforts to implement it.

Alabama	$11,683,635
Georgia	561,490
Georgia-Tennessee[a]	5,232,830
Kentucky	23,797,529
Maryland	473,106
Mississippi	111,470
New York	1,204,951
North Carolina	9,849,164
Ohio	13,086,215
Pennsylvania	1,136,912
South Carolina	16,384,911
Tennessee	1,031,692
Virginia	8,502,379
West Virginia	16,737,338

[a]One 202 area combines counties from these states.

It would be hard to argue on the basis of these figures that a political agency, such as ARC, cannot concentrate funds. There can be no doubt where the commission felt its funds would have the most significant long range impact.

The programs of the 202 areas can be summarized into an emphasis on nine general areas of health care service:

1. Public Health Services
2. Dental Health
3. Environmental Health
4. Home Health Services
5. Health Manpower Development
6. Maternal and Child Care
7. Mental Health and Rehabilitation
8. Intensive Care
9. Communication and Transportation Systems

Not all of these categories of health service delivery are represented in each demonstration area, of course. When account is taken of the paucity of health care services that have existed generally in the region and in the demonstration areas, the programs to make available services of the types just identified would mark a perceptible upward step. Some of the 202 areas engage in mostly traditional activities but others are innovative, for example in the use and training of paraprofessionals. Conceptually, there is probably some limit to the amount of innovation that can be expected in a few years and it is unclear how close the 202 areas may have come to that limit. However, there are two factors, in addition to the one already mentioned, that probably dampened the innovative emphasis of the program.

The first is, again, the personnel decisions of the commission. The 202 program has operated with a very small staff supplemented by borrowed personnel from the Department of Health, Education and Welfare. In total, there has been insufficient staff to even keep all 202 area directors and boards fully informed of the activities of the others. It is not surprising then that there has been little time available for gaining the intimate understanding of each group that might have led to the relaxation of barriers to new thoughts and undertakings. It is unknowable how much might have been accomplished as a result of such contacts but it seems reasonable to expect some impact. Moreover, the procedure for fund allocation provided an opportunity to press for innovation that was, unfortunately, inadequately exploited. Unlike so many other sections of the act, the commission did not originally allocate funds under Section 202 either to states or to demonstration areas. Rather, most of the available funds were kept in a central pool to be allocated on the basis of a competitive evaluation of the proposals received. This process, combined with greater commitment of staff, might have produced a greater acceptance of change.[25]

Another inhibitor of innovation has been the budgetary and project review process. Funds appropriated for Section 202 do not expire at the end of a fiscal year so it might be thought that pressures to close out the account by June 30, the end of the fiscal year, would be absent. This is not the case, however, because carryover funds tend to suggest to appropriations committees that additional funds requested are not fully needed. This leads to pressure to use the available funds and the project review process encourages the submission of orthodox projects. In brief, it takes longer to get approval of a new type of undertaking than for a traditional one. This is to be expected but it serves to dampen innovation nonetheless.

Traditional undertakings lead to the construction of facilities which also have a high appeal locally. They are visible, tangible evidences of contributions to the community from the 202 area board and director. This local appeal would lead to pressure for an emphasis on construction and, undoubtedly, there was need for upgrading of the physical plant in at least parts of the demonstration areas. The review process abetted this, however. It called for sequential reviews by the state agencies concerned, ARC, and one or more federal agencies. Not only was this time-consuming but the more agencies a project must traverse, the more it must be made to resemble the least common denominator acceptable to all of them. To an amazing extent, staff time has been consumed in keeping track of projects and prodding them through the process.

Given the impediments to innovation, it is a compliment to the commission and 202 area staffs involved that as much has been done to make inroads on the shortages of health care personnel that are endemic to the region. Great emphasis in both the 202 and vocational education programs has been given to training activities and novel attempts are being made to economize on the use of trained physicians through the use of nurse practitioners, paraprofessionals, and technological aids. But all combined will not substitute fully for the physician. To encourage more medical students to consider locating in the region, the commission has supported a summer intern program administered by the Student American Medical Association that brings fledgling physicians into the area for a period of apprenticeship and observation. It is too soon to know the long-run fruits of these arrangements but, in the short run, both local practitioners and students claim benefits.

Measuring the impact of a program of enlarged health care delivery is, at best, an uncertain enterprise. The first inclination, to look for changes in mobidity and mortality data, is probably misdirected. Health itself defies measurement and conditions of health are influenced by numerous factors, of which income and nutrition and housing are probably far more influential than health care. Health care is used principally when deviations from accepted standards of health are experienced and even when health is restored, the cause and effect relationship between care and cure may not always be close. Rather, delivering health care is more properly viewed as a goal separate from, but related to, the level of health. It should be evaluated in terms of its own units, the amount of service delivered and its quality. On this score, the record of 202 is impressive. Screening programs have examined over 55,000 people, vaccination programs have reached almost a quarter million, environmental health programs three-quarters of a million.[26] The quality aspects of these programs are unmeasured by these statistics and some, such as the solid waste disposal programs in rural areas, have numerous puzzles that are yet to be solved. But measured in its own terms of service delivery, the 202 program is having effects.

There is one area in which present-day thought establishes an intimate connection between health care and health itself. This is the area of childhood programs for children up to eight years of age. In 1969, Section 202 was broadened to specifically include needs in this age group as well as special programs for "black lung," the chronic affliction of miners. The amendment instructed the commission to develop coordinated programs of child development services that could serve as a model to the rest of the nation.

The need for a coordinated approach was obvious. There exist over 200 federal programs which are supposed to provide services that have beneficial impacts on the health and education of young children. These tend to be fragmented among numerous federal agencies and more numerous state agencies, with the result that services are scattered, spottily available, uncoordinated, and frequently unavailable to rural children. With current thinking emphasizing the close relationship between conditions early in life and later health and performance, a more comprehensive approach seemed mandatory that would narrow the gap between this emerging knowledge and service content and availability. The commission is concentrating its child development program efforts on expanding non-school opportunities for service to children five years of age and younger. (The education program is focusing on the school experience from five to eight.)

In addition to its legislative mandate, the commission had an attractive "carrot" with which to encourage coordinated planning. The Social Security Act reimburses states for 75% of the costs of rendering services to children and provides grants for the training of staff and the revision of programs. However, it provides no funds to support the initiation of such programs. The commission, using funds under Section 202, could provide the initial costs of development, training, and facilities, and of initial operation.

The commission has encouraged the states to plan for a broad range of services to be made available throughout their territory, not just the Appalachian portion. The commission could support service delivery programs only within the region but it encouraged and supported state-wide planning. Most of the available federal programs were already funnelled through state agencies and it seemed wasteful to ask them to think only in terms of their Appalachian areas. Planning grants to the states have been provided to cover the costs of coordinated planning activities by state agencies, with the intention that local groups will be progressively involved in both planning and implementation. It is anticipated that the preparation of these statewide plans will give the Appalachian states an advantage in the future as federal agencies require a more comprehensive approach before disbursing funds.

The commission has set as its objective the development of model child development programs. Its aim is to reach all children (and their families) in an area and provide them with a single entry point from which a wide range of services are to be accessible. These range from family planning to rehabilitation and special education for the handicapped and are designed to serve the physical, emotional, social and education needs of children and their families. By the end of fiscal 1970, all states except Mississippi had received planning grants and their comprehensive child development plans were all due to be submitted by the first of 1972. They were to include lists of projects and other activities to implement them. At that point, operating program funding could begin. $11,500,000 was reserved for this purpose for the last six months of fiscal 1972.

The early actions of the commission in this field are too new to provide a basis for evaluation based on their effects. They have achieved such prominence for their promise however, that the Department of Health, Education and Welfare has asked ARC to coordinate technical assistance to all 50 states as they plan and prepare personnel for child development services. The commission has agreed to undertake this task, one of whose major aims will be to close the gap between the growth of knowledge in this field and its application in service delivery programs.

The day should come when the separate plans being prepared for the state-wide dissemination of child development services are fully compatible with the plans of the 202 areas and the state investment plans. That day is not yet here. In fact, the rationale for preparing statewide child development plans, namely that state agencies are responsible for activities statewide, casts doubt on the rationale for a state investment plan that covers only the Appalachian portion of the state. In the next chapter, there are further comments on the appropriateness of developing regional programs with only parts of states involved.

Supplemental Funds[2][7]

Section 214 contains one of the most innovative concepts included in the Appalachian Act. Under it the commission is given funds to supplement local funds in the financing of grant-in-aid projects so that the local contribution can be reduced to as low as 20% of the project's cost. The basic justification for this provision that was given to the Congress in 1964 and 1965, and later, was that the relatively impoverished communities of the region were unable to participate fully in existing grant-in-aid programs because of their inability to contribute the standard matching share. Therefore, it was argued, special funds were required to supplement local funds and make Appalachian communities competitive for grant programs for construction and original equipment. Progressively, the range of programs that can be supplemented with 214 funds has been broadened but the basic justification has remained the same. There was apparently some justification for this contention. In 1965, the region (with between nine and ten percent of the national population) received about 7.7% of the national construction grants. This has progressively risen until the region's shares of population and grants are about the same. (There is nothing in these figures that can demonstrate either that this has been a movement toward or away from equity or that Section 214 has been an important cause of the change.)

The acceptance of this argument by Congress carried with it a tacit admission. In many, if not most, grant-in-aid formulas, Congress has attempted to relate the availability of federal assistance to some measure of need. However, this has ordinarily been on a statewide basis and there was no way to lighten the burden on any particularly impoverished community or area. Consequently, adoption of Section 214 meant that Congress was recognizing an inadequacy in existing grant-in-aid formulas, though the logic underlying this admission has not yet led to a thorough reconsideration of this aspect of the grant-in-aid approach. Thus far, none of the discussions of revenue sharing have centered upon this problem either.

There are two other major innovative features in Section 214. Congress did not identify specifically which grant-in-aid programs were to be supplemented. Rather it identified a broad list of programs eligible for supplementation. In addition, it permitted latitude in deciding the amount by which the local contribution was to be reduced in each case. In essence, Section 214 gave to the commission an opportunity to experiment with a block grant approach, particularly since the commission did not originally significantly narrow the range of programs that might be eligible for supplementation but left this to be decided by the individual states. The various states differ in the range of federal programs to which 214 funds were applied. They also differ in the techniques employed to determine the recommended local share and the degree to which these shares have been reduced.

Through August, 1971, a total of $214,830,000 had been appropriated for Section 214 and with few exceptions, the commission has still left to the states the decision about which programs each would choose to supplement. Of course the commission maintained the restrictions that individual projects must be justified in the annual state development plan and that, in general, they must be related to the social and economic development of the region. This latter requirement has led to two specific restrictions on the use of Section 214 funds. Because of the great demand for funds to alleviate the shortage of nursing home facilities in the region, the commission decided very early that, to avoid dissipating scarce resources on projects that were worthwhile but generally unrelated to the development of the region, the eligibility of nursing home for supplemental grants was severely limited. For similar reasons, the commission recently concluded that, in general, supplemental grants for law enforcement assistance projects should not be considered because of their low relevance to social and economic development.

Table 8-1 indicates the way in which states divided the funds allocated to them among general program areas through December 31, 1971. Almost 82% of the total was spent on human resource development, an indication of growing commission emphasis on this aspect of the development process. The table also shows how markedly the states differ in the range of federal programs to which 214 funds were applied. For example, Kentucky has spent the bulk of its 214 funds on vocational education, the non-highway program area to which it has given highest priority. Maryland, on the other hand, has concentrated on hospital construction, while Georgia and New York have emphasized sewage treatment facilities.

Through the end of 1972, the states had invested over $185 million of Section 214 funds in various projects. Using the categories of Table 8-1 the distribution of funds was:

Vocational Education	$ 43.2 million
Non-Vocational Education	52.2 million
Health	56.3 million
Water & Sewer	27.3 million
Airports	6.3 million
	185.3 million

Table 8-1
Percent Distribution of Allocated Section 214 Funds

	Vocational Education	Non-Vocational Education	Health	Water & Sewer	Airports
Alabama	27.25	53.34	8.72	10.60	0.08
Georgia	18.57	15.24	21.40	39.76	5.02
Kentucky	53.24	12.60	34.16	0	0
Maryland	14.39	20.85	33.05	30.51	1.21
Mississippi	20.45	45.92	15.09	8.31	10.22
New York	31.12	13.11	33.24	20.82	1.72
North Carolina	31.36	23.29	22.09	21.93	1.32
Ohio	23.74	17.46	39.80	17.03	1.95
Pennsylvania	9.81	26.48	49.94	9.23	4.55
South Carolina	19.31	46.45	5.79	26.79	1.66
Tennessee	16.42	30.34	31.30	17.97	3.96
Virginia	43.22	19.37	28.42	4.53	4.46
West Virginia	23.45	31.24	35.09	2.12	8.10
Region	23.29	28.18	30.36	14.73	3.43

Recent legislative changes have added new dimensions to future operations under Section 214. First, in response to recent airport accidents, the commission was given authority to supplement the cost of airport safety improvements, for which $8.5 million were allocated. Secondly, a whole new opportunity was created. Now funds appropriated under Section 214 can be used to increase the availability of basic federal funds. In other words, Section 214 can be used to supplement the resources of federal agencies as well as those of regional entities. If appropriations to federal agencies do not permit accomplishment of desired developmental projects, the commission may supplement the federal funds. While this is an opportunity, it also contains a danger. In the past, the demand for 214 funds was limited by the availability of basic funds. Now, that automatic limitation on the volume of demand and number of demanders is gone. As a result, the commission is moving very cautiously in using its new authority. It should be noted however, that if 214 appropriations were sufficient (which they are not), this new authority would greatly enhance ARC's ability to direct the flow of federal funds into the region.

Three general conclusions seem warranted. It seems evident from this broadening of authority, that Congress approves of the way in which ARC used its initial authority. It apparently agrees with the greater emphasis that has been given to human resource-related investments. And it certainly appears from the data that the Appalachian states have put a higher value on an additional dollar for human resources investments than for other purposes. This is the genesis of the changing pattern of appropriations among programs discussed in Chapter 6.

A Summary View of Program Investments

A retrospective look at ARC activities in the various functional areas discussed makes evident the extent to which uncertainty has been an ever-present element in the decision process. Not only has there been uncertainty about the proper selection of areas to receive concentrated attention and about the programs most appropriate for each, but there has also been a more pervasive uncertainty whose roots can be found in the discussion in Chapter 4. There the degree of our current understanding of the development process itself was examined. That is the source of the fundamental uncertainty with which those charged with implementing functional programs have to cope.

While groping toward a better understanding of the process, experience has tended to make evident the vast interrelationships in the process. Pragmatically, this has produced a drive toward an increasingly comprehensive approach, evidence of which can be seen in the evolution of several programs. The 202 program and the 211 program began as methods of increasing facility availability for health and vocational education and broadened quickly to include concerns with service delivery and quality. The natural resource programs began as separate activities to remedy individual environmental handicaps in the region and became elements in an attempt at a unified approach to environmental enhancement. Apparently, for the foreseeable future, programs for regional development and narrowly restricted functional program funds will be an increasingly incompatible mixture.

Another look back provides another summary view. In the face of uncertainty, the surest investment is in human resources. No one can know now what the future economic activity or geography or aggregates of economic statistics for the region will look like. Uncertainty pervades the decision concerning which investments, of what scale, sequence and timing, will do most to develop the full potential of a selected area. The most that can be done is to operate on the best information currently available and to recognize that adjustments are most easily made through the mobility of the population. Hence, the emphasis on preparation of the region's citizens to compete for opportunities "wherever they may choose to live." Uncertainty persists but is lessened when the decision is to enhance the inculcated qualities that individuals must possess if they are actually to have options in their decisions about their lives. If for no other reason, a regional development program will be drawn to investments in human resources. By investing heavily in the most mobile form of resources—people—the commission was able to minimize the chance that its investments would be wasted. Though no one could be sure that any particular set of public facility investments could contribute to the development of a self-supporting economy in the more lagging portions of the region, it was clear that better health and education for the people of those areas was a necessary precondition for such development if it was to occur, and, if it did not, individuals could carry them wherever opportunities were available.

The evolution of the program in the face of uncertainty can be traced quantitatively in the requests for funds and the appropriations the program has received. As indicated in Chapter 6, there has been a complete re-orientation of non-highway funds. From PARC's relative preference for physical resource investments, ARC has moved to a 3:1 preference for human resource related investments. And this comparison understates the case because it omits the human resource emphasis with which the general supplementary funds under Section 214 have been allocated.

Undoubtedly, projects and programs would have been administered differently by others from the outset. To this day, there are differences in approach among the participants. Uncertainty is bound to produce such a situation. But uncertainty has also been known to produce rigidity, the substitution of dogmatism for wisdom. Whatever shortcomings there may be in the commission's discharge of its functional responsibilities, it has not fallen prey to this. Despite the discomfiture sometimes produced, it has maintained a willingness to review and adjust its undertakings as insight and experience have been obtained.

9

Appraisal and Prospects

Up to this point the intentions underlying the law and commission policy have been examined at length. Attention has been given to the mechanisms created and the activities undertaken. Now the question is what was the result. This is a complex question to answer and only some aspects of it can be addressed directly. However, the most obvious question is to ask whether the commission placed its projects as it set out to do. This does not attempt to establish the wisdom of the commission's intentions, it only asks if its performance matches its verbiage.

Project Concentration

Naturally, this question was of interest to the commission. It examined the data that summarize its operations and found that they provide an answer that can be summarized under four headings.[1]

1. *The degree of project concentration achieved.* Both the law and the commission code prescribe concentration into growth areas and, despite the exceptions to this requirement summarized in Chapter 5, substantial concentration of projects was achieved in the first five years of the commission's operations. As the following table indicates, 31.5% of the commission's non-highway investments went into 5% of the 397 counties, 55% into 15% of the counties; 30% of the counties received barely more than 1% of the investments and of these counties and 64 received none. The cumulative distribution of counties follows.

These data suggest strongly that there has not been a dominating tendency in the states to follow the politically easy path that leads to a fairly uniform allocation of project monies among all counties.

For many purposes, however, the county is not the most useful geographic unit to use in assessing how funds were distributed geographically. A more useful one, and one that conforms more closely to the commission's present emphasis on the delivery of public services, is to inquire about the degree of proportionality between populations served and funds invested.

2. *The relationship between population and investments.* Commission practices impede easy examination of this aspect of the question. Obviously, projects located in growth areas are designed to serve the populations of those areas. However, as previously noted, commission policy does not require the drawing

153

Table 9-1
Cumulative Investment by County[a]

% of Total Number of Counties	% of Total ARC Investment[b]
5.0	31.5
10.0	45.2
15.0	55.0
20.0	63.9
25.0	70.6
30.0	76.4
40.0	85.6
50.0	92.1
60.0	96.5
70.0	98.9

[a]Counties are arranged according to quantity of ARC investments made, in descending order; i.e., the first 5 percent includes those counties with the highest absolute quantity of ARC investment.
[b]Excluding highway funds.

of precise boundaries around these areas. Consequently, an examination of the state plans will not always yield a list of areas with geographically precise boundaries whose population can then be ascertained. In some states this can be done, in others not.

To overcome this problem, uniform "general service areas" were defined for analytical purposes using the dominant centers or growth areas specified in the state plans. Employing data on population concentration from the 1960 census, newspaper circulation, traffic flow and topographic maps, 173 of these service areas were delineated for the region. They contain 85% of the region's population. The following chart shows the relationship between the share of service area total population and of ARC investments.

Evidently, ARC distributed funds roughly in proportion to population, with two notable exceptions. It put relatively little into the largest area (the one centered on Pittsburgh) and gave greatly disproportionate emphasis to the 44 service areas whose population fell between 10,000 and 25,000. These areas combined contained less than 730,000 people so it is doubtful that vote-seeking was an important factor in the decisions that cumulated to produce this result.

The service areas just examined are analytical ones, not the ones contained in the authoritative statement of the states' intentions, the states' plans. This leads then to the third aspect of the question, did the states achieve concentration in areas as they defined them?

3. *The relationship between growth areas and investments.* Examination of the record on this basis again encounters the problem of non-uniformity among the state plans. This time, it takes the form of differences in terminology in

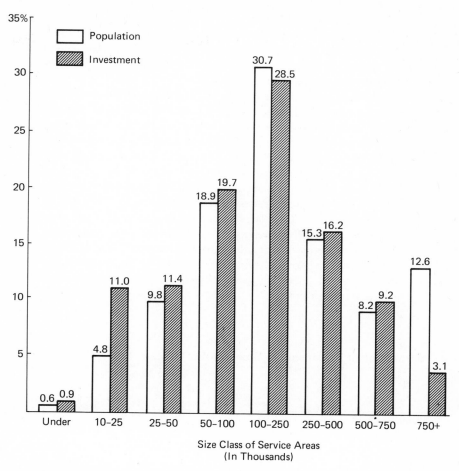

Figure 9–1. Investments (1965–1970) and Population (1960) as Percent of Totals for Service Areas (by Service Area Size Class).

describing growth areas and their potentials. To overcome this, a four-level categorization was created and applied to each state plan. Level 1 was defined as the highest level growth potential in each state and so on down to level 4, areas not designated as growth areas.

A second problem concerned the early "quick-start" period during which investments that were made before growth areas were defined. The data in Table 9-2 do not include those investments nor do they include those funds to which the concentration prescription cannot be applied.

Overall, the data show that over 62% of the investment funds went into the dominant growth areas of each state while almost 14% went into areas not designated as having growth potential. For the region as a whole, a record of reasonable concentration on dominant growth areas has been created but the same cannot be said for some states. Kentucky's low percentage of Level 1 investments is a reflection that it has only one county of a multi-state metropolitan area in its part of Appalachia. The relatively low figures for Georgia, North Carolina and Tennessee reflect state policy decisions to try to foster growth away from their largest centers. By and large, those states with high proportions of Level 4 investments concentrated their available funds on education and health projects using the latitude contained in the ARC code.

Mention of the types of projects involved leads to inquiry about one more aspect of the overall question—what degree of project concentration was achieved in each type of project.

Table 9-2
Concentration of Investments in Growth Areas by State

State	Growth Area Levels			
	1	2	3	4
	(Percent)	(Percent)	(Percent)	(Percent)
Alabama	84.3	1.4	–	14.3
Georgia	33.2	27.1	–	39.7
Kentucky	2.2	45.8	42.0	9.9
Maryland	86.0	14.0	–	–
Mississippi	87.2	6.9	–	5.9
North Carolina	17.3	36.5	43.4	2.8
New York	80.5	9.9	–	9.6
Ohio	87.2	9.7	–	3.1
Pennsylvania	86.1	4.8	2.9	6.2
South Carolina	68.6	9.1	–	21.3
Tennessee	38.7	26.5	24.3	10.5
Virginia	61.5	–	–	38.5
West Virginia	67.3	3.0	9.5	20.2
Region	62.1	13.9	10.3	13.7

4. *Project concentration by type of project.* Table 9-3 summarizes the answer to this aspect of the question. Projects are categorized into five groups and in each, with the exception of water and sewer projects, half or more of the funds went into the highest level, 70% or more of the funds into the two highest level areas. The exception is an interesting one because it reflects the difference of opinion that has characterized commission and staff discussions from the beginning. Some have viewed water and sewer projects as a necessary component of the commission's program to upgrade health levels. They would therefore permit quite wide latitude to the states in locating them under the exceptions to the rules on concentration. Others view them as necessary components of the program to improve the public facilities available at selected locations. Recognizing that funds for these purposes under the act were limited, they urged that they be conserved for use at these locations, with other places getting their support from other programs. The data reflect the see-saw nature of the conclusions to these discussions.

Returning to the original, and narrow, question with which this discussion began, the answer apparently is more affirmative than negative. The commission did succeed during its first five years of operation in placing projects in general conformity with its intentions. Another question is whether having been so located, did they serve the purposes of the program, a question whose answer must be largely judgmental but that does depend somewhat on knowing the recent trends of conditions in Appalachia.

Indicators of Change

Early in this book, in Chapter 3, a description of some of the dimensions of the Appalachian problem was presented as the background for later discussion and as an explanation for the passage of the Appalachian legislation. Now it seems

Table 9-3
Expenditures by Growth Area Level and Investment Category (in percent)

Investment Category	Growth Area Levels				
	1	2	3	4	Total
Health	50.0	18.7	14.0	17.3	100.0
Education	61.6	15.5	9.5	13.4	100.0
Water & Sewer	46.7	14.1	10.7	28.5	100.0
Airport	64.2	12.2	13.2	10.4	100.0
Other	50.9	20.0	21.1	8.0	100.0
Total[a]	57.2	15.9	10.6	16.3	100.0

[a]Note the percentage distribution of this row is not equal to the distribution in the preceding table. This is due to the removal of access roads and mine area restoration projects included in the preceding table because lack of data did not permit their inclusion here.

reasonable to ask, what has happened in more recent years? In those broad aggregates with which we deal with individuals, how have Appalachians been faring?

Humanity and curiosity lead to these questions and their answer should not imply that changes noted are ascribable to the Appalachian program. Some may be, but we really do not know which, if any, or how much. Rather, the changes are coincident with, rather than due to, the program and reflect forces beyond its control. This is particularly true of the regional impacts of national policies,[3] about which too little is known. To unmeasured degrees, Appalachia's condition benefitted from national prosperity and suffered from credit stringency and recession.

Three commonly used statistics tell the story of events in the region—population change, income, and employment and unemployment—and all repeat the refrain of variability within the region.

In the 1960's, Appalachia's population increased by 2.7%, faster than its 1950-1960 growth of 2% but still much less than the national growth of 13.3% for the 1960's. This population performance can be explained by three factors: a) the region's age distribution shows relatively fewer residents in the child-bearing years, largely due to earlier out-migration; b) a decline in the birth rate, coincident with the same event nationally; and c) continued out-migration. Net out-migration, at 1.1 million, is down considerably from the 2.2 million of the preceding decade.

Only one state's Appalachian portion, Georgia's, had net inmigration and in one, Ohio, net out-migration exceeded the 1950-60 rate. This is part of an overall pattern that shows virtual population stability in the northern part of the region, population losses in the central part, and population gains in the southern part. (Employment data mirror this pattern.) Over 40% of the region's net out-migration occurred from Kentucky, Pennsylvania and West Virginia.

Within this population pattern, there is also an urbanizing pattern. As Table 9-4 shows, of the region's 140 counties without any urban area, 109 were either stable or lost population and in its 116 most moderately urban counties, 63 could be similarly described. In its 58 metropolitan and other highly urbanized counties, 27 were stable or lost population. In the mid-range, 83 counties with urban populations of 10,000 to 50,000, 38 were stable or had population losses. Overall, 63 of the region's 397 counties lost more than 10% of their population in the decade and an additional 63 lost 5% or more of their population. The group showing the most consistent pattern of growth is the group of counties with moderate urban populations in the 10,000-25,000 range.

Between 1962 and 1968, the region's personal income grew by a bit more than half, producing a notable increase in per capita income when combined with the slow population growth just noted. Compared to the nation, progress toward equalization in percentage terms occurred. The region's 1962 per capita income of $1,791 was 75.1% of the U.S. figure of $2,368. By 1968, the U.S. per

Table 9-4
Population Changes in Appalachian Counties by Urban Classification: 1960-1970

Urban Size Classification	Pop. Increased over 11.7%	Pop. Increased from 1.0% to 11.7%	Pop. Changed + or − less than 1%	Pop. Declined −1.0% to −5.0%	Pop. Declined −5.0% to −10.0%	Pop. Declined −10.0% to −20.0%	Pop. Declined over −20.0%	Total
Class 5	8	16	4	13	3	1	–	45
Class 4	–	7	1	1	4	–	–	13
Class 3	4	6	4	3	6	–	–	23
Class 2	13	22	8	6	6	4	1	60
Class 1	18	35	8	22	16	11	6	116
Class 0	8	23	11	30	28	35	5	140
Total	51	109	36	75	63	51	12	397

Urban Size Classification of Counties Based on 1960 Population:

Class 5 – SMSA's

Class 4 – 50,000 and Over Urban Population

Class 3 – 25,000 to 49,999 Urban Population

Class 2 – 10,000 to 24,999 Urban Population

Class 1 – 2,500 to under 10,000 Urban Population

Class 0 – No Urban Population – Entirely Rural

Source: *Five Years in Appalachia*, Executive Director's Annual Report, July 1-Dec. 31, 1970, p. 38.

capita income had grown to $3,425 and the region's was 78.8% of this, at an absolute level of $2,698. Although the Appalachian income per person is now close to four-fifths the national figure, the absolute difference has grown. $577 separated the two figures in 1962, by 1968 the difference was $727.

Each of the four major sub-regions showed changes in per capita personal income that narrowed the differential in percentage terms. But in each case, in absolute terms the gap is greater. The narrowing has been in the range of two to three percentage points but it is the absolute differences that measure the relative levels of living attained. Table 9-5 shows these differences but understates them because the U.S. figure is biased downward by the inclusion of Appalachian statistics in the total U.S. data.

If one moral can be drawn from these data, it is the long road of rapid change that will have to occur in Appalachia before its average level of living approximates that of the nation.

Change is taking place, though more slowly than hoped, as the data on unemployment and employment reveal. In 1960, when the average unemployment rate in the rest of the country was 5.0%, the figure PARC computed for Appalachia was 7.1%. In 1969, before the full impact of the recession was felt, the regional rate exceeded the national by only 0.4 of a percentage point. Partly, this is a reflection of out-migration but employment growth contributed to it.

With the exception of mining, regional employment is growing. The sub-parts are all experiencing employment growth also but relatively greater increases have occurred in the region's central and southern states.[4] The pattern is one of manufacturing growth (and by far not all low wage manufacturing) both seeking and stimulating the emerging urban markets away from the established centers. The emerging centers tend to also show strength in some non-manufacturing sectors. The older, more established northern centers are having competitive difficulties.

Overall, the employment changes do not suggest a rapid regional convergence

Table 9-5
Per Capita Personal Income

	1962	Difference from U.S.	1968	Difference from U.S.
U.S.	$2,368		$3,425	
Appalachia	1,791	$ 577	2,698	$ 727
Northern	2,066	302	2,997	428
Central	1,140	1,218	1,728	1,701
Southern	1,649	719	2,475	950
Highlands	1,574	794	2,356	1,069

Source: Data provided by Office of Business Economics, U.S. Department of Commerce to ARC.

Table 9-6
Rates of Increase in Covered Employment[a] 1965-1969

	U.S.	Appalachia	Central[b] Appalachia	Southern[b] Appalachia	Northern[b] Appalachia
Total	18	16	21	20	11
Manufacturing	17	11	29	19	7
Contract Construction	14	13	28	14	34
Mining	0	−10	−12	13	− 9
Wholesale Trade	14	14	20	12	14
Retail Trade	19	16	17	16	16
Transportation and Public Utilities	15	13	22	23	9
Finance, Insurance and Real Estate	26	26	33	30	22

[a]Estimates based on reports from state bureaus of employment security.

[b]For this table, Central Appalachia means the regional portions of Kentucky, Tennessee and Virginia; Southern Appalachia means Alabama, Georgia and Mississippi, North Carolina and South Carolina; and Northern Appalachia, the balance of the region.

Source: Computed from *Five Years in Appalachia*, Section on Economic Report, pp. 10-19 and Appendix.

to the national employment pattern with its more modest dependence on manufacturing as a source of jobs. An identical employment structure is probably in the interest of neither the region nor the nation but movement to greater similarity may be underway. Both are becoming less dependent on manufacturing for jobs. The region's dependence on manufacturing fell from 46.5% of the total to 45.7% between 1965 and 1969 while for the U.S. the decline was from 36.9% to 35.9%.

Returning to the question that opened this section, on the average Appalachians are doing better but (by national standards) still not well. The averages hide quite a range and there are still too many Appalachians whose economic condition does not conform to our accepted standards of adequacy, or even of decency.

Impact of Activities

The commission has understood that the data just presented could not be taken as a measure of the impact of its activities. It also realized that many of the consequences of its activities would have delayed effects and that some of these effects are unmeasurable by presently available techniques. However, it still wanted some insight into the reactions to its activities in local areas. Its principal motivation was a desire to understand the regional development process better and to get a fuller sense of the impact it may have been having. Consequently, the commission sponsored a series of interviews with leaders in centers which had received relatively large concentration of ARC funds for a variety of projects. It was understood at the outset that the results of the inquiry would have to be assessed carefully. Talking to government, industrial and community leaders does not provide a full sample of community opinion, particularly when those interviewed are aware that their responses will be relayed to the organization which has been providing substantial financial support. In addition, in all of the communities sampled, ARC was decidedly not the sole agency making funds available, so the impact of ARC-sponsored investments would be intermixed with that of others. Overall, it was understood that the effects of public investments might take longer to be felt than the short time since ARC began making funds available, and that the causal connection between public actions and private responses is not precisely known.

In no sense were the communities studied chosen because they were "typical" of the centers of growth areas in the region. As a result, it was understood in advance that generalization from their experiences would be hazardous. The decision to proceed with the study was based on the hope that it might throw some light on the issue of whether concentration of public investments in these communities resulted in ramifications beyond the impacts of the individual projects involved. Proof of the existence of synergistic effect could not be established from this study but if its absence were noted, doubts would be raised about a basic presupposition of the program. The entire effort was based on an expectation that concentration of investments would permit some communities to become the focus of wider public and private opportunities for their citizens and those of the surrounding area.

Seven communities were selected because of the magnitude of the investments they had received and also because they were geographically dispersed and had experienced divergent patterns of performance. Summary data, indicating the nature of ARC investments and the communities' population and income performance, are given in Table 9-7.[5]

All seven communities had received assistance for water or sewer projects and all except Carrollton had been helped to expand their health care facilities. Cookeville is the only one that did not get assistance for vocational education. Both Hornell and Altoona lost population in the last decade and these are the only two whose income, relative to the U.S. fell during the period. All seven communities are on either interstate or development highways.

It was not a principal aim of the study to examine the utilization of the facilities supported but, inevitably, information on this subject was gathered. Two related points were commonly made. Utilization of facilities tended to exceed expectations so that capacity intended to satisfy later expansion of demand was used rather promptly. The commonly given explanation for this, which is the second point, was that the service area of the community had been

Table 9-7
Selected Growth Centers: Basic Characteristics and Composition and Value of Investment Package

Center	County	Population 1970*	Population % Change 60-70	Total Project Cost ($000)	ARC Investment ($000)	Number and Type of Project # 1 2 3 4 5 6 7	Per Capita Income 1959	Per Capita Income 1968	Percent of U.S. 1959	Percent of U.S. 1968	% Change 59-68
Hornell, N.Y.	Steuben	11,979	−13.9	$ 6,654.5	$1,744.5	4 x x x	$2074	$3122	96.0	91.3	50.5
Gaffney, S.C.	Cherokee	12,868	23.3	2,147.4	1,157.4	5 x x x x x	1240	2063	57.4	60.3	66.4
Cookeville, Tenn.	Putnam	14,205	82.0	8,878.1	1,116.0	7 x x x	1105	2005	51.5	58.6	81.4
Crossville, Tenn.	Cumberland	5,267	12.8	2,436.7	904.4	5 x x x x x	825	1596	38.2	46.7	93.4
Altoona, Pa.	Blair	133,973	− 2.4	10,953.4	1,639.7	6 x x x x x x	1811	2797	83.8	81.8	54.4
Florence, Ala.	Lauderdale	33,535	6.0	11,490.7	3,281.3	11 x x x x x x x	1234	1995	57.1	58.3	61.7
Carrollton, Ga.	Carroll	13,325	21.4	6,577.7	1,785.3	7 x x x x x x x	1291	2170	59.7	63.4	68.1
Total				$49,138.5	$11,628.6						

*Preliminary reports from 1970 census

Type of Project
1 - Health
2 - Vocational Education
3 - Higher Education
4 - Airport
5 - Library
6 - Sewer and Water
7 - Other: Recreation, Housing, Access Road

enlarged by transportation improvements and by the very existence of the service, which led more people to come to the city when that service was desired. Apparently, at least in these communities, it has been possible to enlarge the hinterland for which a center is the service delivery focus.

Not unexpectedly, local leaders emphasized the impact of projects on the economic performance of their communities. Generally, they reflected an understanding of the industrial location process. They recognized that no single factor, such as transportation or labor costs, was the key to economic growth but that a combination of factors was at work. Moreover, they realized that many locations can provide an employer with roughly equal costs and that the final decision is influenced by intangible items such as community attitudes, the quality of local leadership, the quality of the living environment, and community appearance. Many of the interviews dwelled on these latter factors as local people sought to verbalize the impact of public investments on the economy and general character of the communities. Frequently, the arrival of new firms, new locators, and expansions of existing ones, were explained by these factors. The closing of existing firms was typically associated either with personal considerations or national economic conditions. Whether or not these explanations are empirically valid, they are indicative of the attitudes toward their communities that were protrayed.

In summarizing the results of this aspect of the study, the commission report said: The characteristics that must be present for growth potential to exist include: (1) a labor force of sufficient size, diversity, and skill to attract new activities; (2) a surplus of developable sites for location and expansion of economic activities; (3) an attractive living environment which includes competitive levels of community services and facilities; (4) accessibility to a sufficient size market and resource base to support a growing economy; (5) proximity to a major metropolitan area which can supply at some minimum level of effort, cultural and other services to local residents and businesses not normally available in a center of its size; and (6) a modern governmental and financial structure.[6]

The relative importance of these factors will differ among locations. In the selected centers studied, two conditions appear to have been principally responsible for their success or lack of success in achieving their respective economic and service potentials. These are multidirectional highway access within their service area connecting the center to areas of greater economic importance, and progressive local leadership.

Appreciative comments about the appearance of the new facilities and their marked contrast to the older buildings and the older community in general were common. Frequently, the new structures were identified as samples of what the community would become. However, enthusiasm of community leaders is not enough to create growth and development. The sentiment must pervade the community sufficiently to provide the political and financial support that community upgrading requires. Therefore, the interviews sought evidence of the degree of popular support that existed.

In most of the communities examined, evidence of community support could be found. Frequently, it was found in the political process. Candidates associated with wide-ranging programs of community improvement, even though they were associated with higher local costs, were winning over those associated with the more passive policies followed in the recent past. In general, the groups receiving support advocated change and sought it, while those defeated tended to behave as though they grudgingly accepted it, if thrust upon them. There tended to be growing community support for planning and priority-setting over a wide range of services and facilities, and including neighboring areas. The cities studied tended to recognize a need for systematic examination of their needs and options, perhaps because they saw the tangible fruits of the planning that preceded the recent facility construction. By and large, they were well aware of the variety of sources of external funding available to them, a factor which may explain the political support new leadership tended to receive.

The process by which a community sets its priorities is a complex blend of needs that are evident to the outsider and those that satisfy local longings whose importance to the community would be missed by someone not immersed in its values. The commission study made no attempt to evaluate the appropriateness of the projects the communities sought. Rather, inquiry was directed at two related points. First, interviewees were asked about the effect of ARC fund availability on the relative priority of projects. Uniformly, the response was that basic priorities had not been altered but that, as is always true, when funds for a more desired project were unavailable, it was put aside temporarily to take advantage of funds that were available for other projects. In effect, this meant that grant fund availability might alter the sequence of expenditures but it did not lead to an alteration of the overall project priority list. Secondly, communities were asked about the financial impact of ARC funds on local finances. In no case was there evidence that local effort had been diminished through the substitution of grant funds for local monies. Rather, local financial effort seemed to be larger, a reflection of the general support for community improvement previously noted.

The study of these seven communities left a strong impression on the researcher that an important by-product of the individual investments, one that probably only resulted because of their concentration in time and place, was a change in the community's attitudes and behavior toward itself. This confirms earlier research, covering some of the same communities, and implies that they are now better able to provide the intangibles required for an expansion of economic activity and of a service delivery role to adjacent areas as well as the tangible requirements.

Generalization far beyond the seven communities studied would be hazardous for all the reasons previously given. Moreover, the effect on these seven may have been partly due to the fact that similarly concentrated investments were not being made in other communities in their immediate vicinity. It does seem reasonable to conclude, however, that nothing from the study tends to cast doubt on the expectation that concentration of investments will have mutually reinforcing effects on a community.

What Have We Learned?

The key question to be asked is whether the Appalachian Act's development strategy, and the instruments to implement it, have been successful. It may be interesting to note, as preceding pages of this chapter have done, that the commission has generally conformed to its own policy guidelines, that the region's economic performance is better than it was, and that communities that receive a good deal of assistance are encouraged by it. None of these, however, are directly responsive to the key question. They provide tangential insight and shed light on the setting in which the program operated but not more than this.

Our present capabilities do not permit a full answer to the question.[7] There are several traditional methods of inquiry designed for use in answering comparable questions. The use of controlled experiments, so useful in many physical science fields, is unavailable here, as it is in most social science investigations. Cost-benefit and cost effectiveness analysis, so useful in many social science inquiries, as well as in the physical sciences, are not applicable. Their application requires a degree of understanding of causal connections between actions and effects that has yet to be attained. The brief time since the program's initiation militates against the use of the traditional social science approaches of time and trend analyses.

It simply must be accepted that we cannot and will not know answers to two questions that are most important:

1. What would Appalachia have been like had no special program been enacted? This is the ubiquitous "with-and-without" question that is so frequently confused with "before-and-after."
2. What would the effect on the region have been if similar amounts had been spent in alternative ways under other programs, or differing amounts on the existing or other programs?

There is a third question of great importance about the national fortune whose answer is beyond our grasp. How might the national welfare have been affected by alternative program designs or funding—or no program at all?

None of these questions lead to definite answers but the Appalachian experience does provide some hints at potential strategies for use on other national issues and some suggestions of new areas for intellectual inquiry. At most, these can be offered tentatively, in the hope that other experiences and insights will be compared to them so that all may be sharpened in the process.

Any survey of contemporary national problems—moral, legal, fiscal, environmental, institutional, political—should be sufficiently humbling that no one can pretend to offer a solution. It is trite to note that it took a long time to create any given problem and (by a strange jump in logic) "therefore" it will take considerable time to overcome it. More accurately, problems of the type we face are rarely solved or "overcome," regardless of our ideological support for the anthem of civil rights. Rather, we mitigate, we ameliorate, we set in motion a process that strives to diminish harsh impacts while we learn more about the problem, as well as the untoward and unexpected impacts of our attempts at "solution."

This view of our approach to social problems places special emphasis on the procedure for handling them that is instituted. The procedure established is important because it can foster or impede the pragmatic adapability that is required as problems are better understood and the impacts of programs are perceived. This view argues that the procedure selected conditions the ultimate effect—that there is a public policy counterpart to the much touted notion that "the medium is the message."

Acceptance of this procedure-oriented viewpoint leads to an emphasis on institution-building and institutional performance. It seeks to find and build public and private organizations and mechanisms whose structure and processes seem well-adapted to the task to be performed. At this time, there are no abstract principles by which the alternative institutions can be judged, though there are notions and insights. Basically, evaluation of their suitability finally depends on their results. "By their fruits ye shall know them." But as was just noted, all the results of the Appalachian effort are not available for inspection. Instead of an inductive basis for judgment—evaluating an organization on the basis of its results—a deductive process will have to serve as a proxy. The question then becomes are there social issues of national concern for which the procedure embodied in the Appalachian effort might be judged a useful approach.

Though it has many sub-parts that are sometimes viewed as separate problems, there is a general set of issues that are frequently subsumed in a plea for a national growth policy. President Nixon had a group working on this policy question[8] and made it a central point in his 1970 State of the Union address. He pointed to our lack of general national goals and objectives that would give substance to the oft-repeated hope for "rural-urban balance," maximize opportunities for residents of all areas of the country, and reverse the deterioration of our environment. The topic has been emphasized in scholarly discussions. It has been the subject of several executive and legislative reports.[9] There has been a spate of bills introduced into Congress designed, in one way or another, to specify the objectives we should seek or, far more frequently, establish programs to accomplish some element of an unspecified grand design for the national future.

In the absence of a clearer specification of objectives, it is difficult to know precisely the aims toward which public policy is moving but it seems reasonable to suggest some of the objectives that might be sought. They relate to opportunities for gainful employment in rural and urban areas, the quality and availability of education and health services, pollution abatement and environmental quality, effective law enforcement, reasonable access to high speed ground and air transport, and recreational opportunities in both urban and rural settings. This list of objectives is a distillation, or partial compilation, of the objectives contained in some of the several hundred grant-in-aid programs now in existence. In establishing these programs, the Congress has announced a national interest in the attainment of their purposes, so it cannot be said that we have no national objectives. It is more accurate to say that our objectives have been established on a piecemeal basis and that, as a result, there is a strong likelihood that they may be inconsistent, and leave some important matters untouched, that the mechanisms established may be duplicative, and that there may be gaps in the availability of programs to achieve them.

In Chapter 3 it was pointed out that part of the rationale for the Appalachian Act was the failure of the grant-in-aid approach to serve the region's needs adequately. Dissatisfaction goes far beyond the region's borders, however, so that there is now an apparent and growing consensus that there is need for a basic overhaul.[10] In thinking about the alternatives available, it is well to have in mind the shortcomings commonly attributed to the present arrangements. The following problems can be identified:

1. Individual grant programs, each designed to satisfy a specific need, almost inevitably do not cover all geographic areas or all aspects of the general problem. This leads to confusion and to discontent due to the apparent inconsistencies or inequities.
2. Separate programs covering related or identical problems, enacted at different times, lead almost inevitably to fragmentation of responsibility among several agencies, each with its own rules and procedures.
3. Each program usually and properly requires the preparation of some type of plan to justify or explain the benefit to be derived from the federal support. However, these planning activities tend to be uncoordinated and in some cases inconsistent, leading to duplication of effort, still further confusion, and charges of bureaucracy, red tape and incompetence.
4. Numerous and conflicting planning requirements may restrict the availability of some programs in areas or communities that are otherwise deserving but lack the skill, endurance or funds to meet them.
5. For numerous programs, the geographic area of responsibility of the planning agency does not cover the entire area which should be included in the plans, if the programs designed are to be as efficient as possible.

6. The availability of federal funds for narrowly specified purposes serves as a lure to state and local governments. They are led to appropriate their matching share even though other needs, for which no federal funds are available, might have a higher priority.

7. For those federal programs that accept localities as applicants, a local-federal relationship develops that bypasses the intermediate level of government, the states, and does not take advantage of the vantage point the states could provide. In effect, the federal agencies attempt to make judgments about local circumstances. In fact, they are frequently too remote to perceive fully the ramifications of their actions.

8. For those federal programs that require state participation and approval, there is no mechanism at the state or federal level which is required, by federal law, to effectively assure consistency among plans and programs. In practice, state agencies develop close relationships with their federal counterparts and at neither level of government is there a mechanism which guards against offsetting activities among programs or activities which are based upon differing goals.

A suggestion sometimes advanced is that some of these problems could be eliminated if all programs related to a given type of facility or service were combined, ending duplication and gaps in availability. There is apparent logic to this suggestion and it might sometimes be helpful if implemented. The suggestion would have all water pollution abatement assistance combined in one program, for example, or place all programs concerned with community water and effluent treatment under one administering body. However, it does not deal with one important reason why numerous programs to serve the same general needs were enacted in the first place.

In a nation as large and diverse as ours, several approaches may be necessary to achieve a given objective. To continue the example, the water and water-related requirements of a metropolitan area, their costs, problems, alternatives, and effects are only vaguely related to those in a semi-rural or rural area. Separate programs were established in partial recognition of this—and geographic overlaps and gaps were the result. However, merely consolidating them into one program is not a fully effective answer. There are substantive differences that have to be handled. In different parts of the country, the means for achieving a given objective may be vastly different. This is true comparing rural and urban, it is also true comparing East with Midwest and West. Unitary programs might compound the existing rigidities.

The grant-in-aid approach also leads to an inflexibility of priorities. Once Congress has established national priorities by appropriating money for a certain functional program (perhaps to several agencies), there is no reasonable way to obtain an adjustment of priorities for a state or area whose priority needs may differ markedly from the national "average," on the basis of which Congress acted. This is the source of the fairly common complaint that Congress is determining state and local priorities and appropriations. Once a grant-in-aid program is established, pressures develop (as Congress intended) to use it. These pressures lead to the appropriation of funds by states and localities to cover their matching share. Any legislator or budget officer will testify that the "multiplier" on local funds (three federal dollars for each local one in a 75-25 matching program) makes it far easier to obtain funds for matching purposes than for other needs for which no matching funds from Washington are available. Inevitably, higher priority goes to those purposes for which grants are available. This is what was intended. However, it would be only a rare coincidence if both the programs pursued and pace of expenditures stimulated were to match the patterns of activities and spending that Congress would have legislated had it been fully aware of the local situation.

Congress must legislate without full knowledge of the specific impacts of its laws. National policies and national goals can have different implications for various parts of the country. For example, the national policy of the Homestead Act, with its 160 acre limitation, was appropriate for areas conducive to intensive agriculture but had undesired effects in areas best suited to extensive agriculture. The national formula for distribution of highway trust funds produced such a mismatch of funds and needs that the Appalachian Development Highway System was conceived to remedy the effects. The interstate highway system has been a boon to the rural resident and the bane of metropolitan central cities. At a lower level of generalization, it is unlikely to be wise policy everywhere to lure local funds into vocational school construction without assessing the relative needs for other educational (and non-educational) facilities and services. The same can be said about the benefits from advanced stages of effluent treatment (now required) compared to abating other environmental degradation or from expenditures on health and other social needs generally.

The case is not being made however, for an abrogation of Congress' responsibility to establish national objectives. There is a national stake in the social, economic, physical, political and environmental health of our citizens. The proposals for giving block grants to states through such devices as revenue sharing seem ill-conceived for precisely this reason. By going to the extreme of distributing virtually untied funds to the States, advocates of revenue sharing are announcing that national objectives are not more than a sum of local and state objectives. This assumes a highly reliable local and state decision process as well as an insularity and lack of mobility of the population that is inconsistent for a president who made the need for a national growth policy the theme of his 1970 State of the Union address.

One contemporary example may be sufficient to indicate why national goals are not the sum of local priorities. It is now generally accepted that in the competitive race to secure new manufacturing plants, the various lures offered by the states cancel each other. If all states stopped their offers, their relative positions would remain virtually unchanged but as long as any one state engages in these financial attraction devices, all feel compelled to do so. If one state were to use the funds obtained from revenue sharing to augment its industrial attraction activities, all would feel compelled to do so. The result of revenue sharing would then be a redistribution of benefits that Congress, from a national standpoint, never could have accepted. Other examples, relating to the health, education and welfare of the people, could be offered but the point may be clear. There is a national point of view, leading to national objectives, that can not be distilled from a compilation of local and state objectives.

The problem therefore is to find a means to accommodate the flexibility needed to reflect the local situation, which grants-in-aid cannot do very well, and the desire to establish national priorities, which revenue sharing cannot do very well. The Appalachian experience may offer a useful alternative.

A program that blends national objectives and local priorities could be modelled after the form of the Appalachian Commission. In strict voting terms, it could be designed to foster accommodation between state and federal interests. More importantly, the idea of the state plan is crucial. It could be the means through which the states determine the significance of a wide range of programs for specific areas of their state. They would rank the problems and opportunities they deem it most important to address and specify the programs that are relevant to them. So, if a state determined that it preferred junior college development to airport development, it could allocate federal funds accordingly. In making these determinations, however, the range of options available to the state could be limited. First, and most apparent, there could be limitations written into law that restrict discretion in allocating funds. Equally important and less apparent, would be the limits imposed by the policy constraint of the federal vote. The federal vote is designed to ultimately insure that all the options for spending federal funds among which the states choose are acceptable from a national policy point of view. In a sense, therefore, the regional commission is a half-way house between grants-in-aid and revenue sharing as a means of addressing social questions.

The overall administrative arrangement might consist of six to eight regional commissions encompassing all states, each composed of whole states, designed to avoid dividing metropolitan areas as much as possible, and each consisting of the governors (with 50% of the vote) and a single federal representative. Fund allocations among states would be a commission responsibility, constrained by a requirement of equitability among states and among the urban, suburban and rural areas within each state.

Congress would still specify national objectives (for example, one might be to make vocational education at the high school and post-high school level available for all who qualify and choose to seek it) but it would leave to the states, with commission sanction, decisions about the relative emphasis on various goals. The states and the commission would have to establish priorities among goals.

Congress would have to specify the minimum progress it expected toward each goal over a five or ten year period but it would leave sufficient latitude, hopefully, for selective advance toward them and for alternative approaches to them. The federal representatives' principal responsibility would be to insure that the national purposes were being served.

At the present time, expenditure of grant funds is a state and local operation, supervised from afar by federal agencies. That supervisory role would continue but decisions about the suitability of projects would fall upon the states, subject to commission approval. Probably no state is now equipped to make the multi-program priority judgments that would be required. The existing grant-in-aid approach has not fostered this decision capability and the operations of the Appalachian Commission do not provide only favorable experience from which to project the possible results of a broadened application. Preceding pages have noted major instances in which expectations have not been satisfied. And the gap between expectation and performance is perhaps the greatest in the realm of state planning and administration. However, this weakness is not avoided by revenue sharing. Both alternatives to the grant-in-aid approach place heavy reliance on the wisdom and abilities of state government. Apparently, the issue of improving state competency cannot be avoided, if it is granted that an alternative to the grant-in-aid approach is needed.

The revenue sharing approach, as proposed by the president, offers no direct incentives to better planning, management or program development. The quality of state administration is assumed to be of concern to the people of the state and no one else, despite the fact that federal funds are being spent. The regional commission approach offers at least a mechanism for expressing a continuing national concern and hopefully, would lead to progressively higher standards of expected attainment before federal funds would continue to be made available to the states. The Appalachian experience suggests that there may be a direct relationship between the amount of money available to a state and the attention that planning for its use receives. A larger federal program might hasten qualitative improvements in state performance if the availability of money was tied to increasingly rigorous standards of performance. Moreover, experience in Appalachia suggests that the availability of a commission staff, partially paid by the states, makes the states more willing to accept technical assistance that would be rejected from strictly federal sources.

Quite clearly, the Appalachian experience does not offer a panacea for the solution of the social issues of concern. However, of the other available alternatives, revenue sharing and a continuation of the grant-in-aid approach, it may be the one with the least flaws. It builds in a pragmatic flexibility and innovative potential and has marshalled a rather remarkable degree of political support.[11]

Whether or not the institutional attributes of the Appalachian effort are adapted to wider-ranging public purposes, the conceptual uncertainties that have dogged the Appalachian Commission will continue to be bothersome. At both the federal and state level, consciously or unconsciously, decisions will continue to be made that affect the social and economic well-being of the people in different areas in different ways. Therefore, aside from any institutional insights arising from the activities of the last six years, conceptual insights and information gained may also be important.

In the years since PARC's activities, literally millions of dollars have been spent by numerous federal agencies, regional commissions, private groups, states, and others to add to our understanding of the regional development process. Rather than creating some fundamentally new concept of the process, intellectual progress has largely consisted of efforts to understand more fully the concepts discussed previously and their relationships to each other. Insights therefore have been small increments to understanding, not leaps forward, a situation that is frustrating both to the analyst and the policy-maker.

These years have seen the generation and distribution of far more data about regional events than was available before. Analytical data series on income, labor force mobility, inter-industry relationships, and public expenditures, to name only some, are now in existence for some or all of the relatively small parts of the country. They permit the statistical testing of hypotheses about which only conjecture was possible before. Despite this, and as every researcher discovers, there are still gaps in the data and inconsistencies among series that impede their fullest use. To cite one example, it is still impossible to get a statistical series on the flow of capital expenditures by public bodies in a specified geographic area. Since so much of our regional development policy depends upon the assumption that changing public service facility availability can have desired causal effects, the absence of this information is obviously damaging to further research and understanding. Another, and very basic inadequacy of the data base for further work arises from the fact that most of our information about public activities is measured in input terms, usually financial (dollars invested in pollution abatement facilities) or physical (new hospital beds available), when what we really want to know is the effect of the new activity on the quantity and quality of service delivered. We are just on the verge of establishing systems to garner the most useful output measures, indexes of the quantity and quality of services delivered.

Existing, but unavailable information is, of course, useless. The awareness of this led to the marked emphasis in the last few years on the creation of data systems that will make timely information available for program administration and research purposes. Forces far more powerful than those generated out of the Appalachian and other area and regional development efforts lie behind this emphasis but they have and will facilitate developmental efforts. The time is at hand, for instance, when someone in a governor's office can have available meaningful summary statistics about activities throughout state government as they affect various areas of the state. The relationship between these activities and issues of social concern, such as health or housing, can be displayed and analyses performed. There can be no assurance that a tool of this nature will be used for program management but not too many years ago the desire to use it would have been stymied by its unavailability. These same data systems cannot always provide information tailored to the needs of research, since data requirements for the two purposes are not identical, but there is a marked overlap and a mine of data for analytical purposes will develop as these systems are in existence for more and more years.

Among the fruits of the efforts of the last several years have been some shifts in understanding about various aspects of the process of regional development. Though it had been known that migration tended to involve relatively young adults and the better educated, more is now known about the characteristics of these migrants, their origins and destinations, the inducements to mobility, and the phenomenon of reverse migration. Only meager additional insight has been gained about the flows of capital among areas and the role of various financial institutions in affecting and creating those flows. We do, however, now have a somewhat clearer picture of the extent to which areas of distress use their capital and of the mechanisms by which it flows. Recent years have seen an alteration in the understanding of the role that natural resources play in the development process. There is continued assurance that natural resource extraction is a meager and uncertain basis for an expanding economic future but natural resources and recreation as amenity attractions to industry and population have received increasing emphasis and specification. Coupled with concern about environmental issues, this has given a natural resource emphasis to attempts to understand area prospects that probably could not have been predicted even five years ago.

Part of this natural resource emphasis has flowed from the efforts expended to understand the industrial location process more fully. For some time it has been apparent that manufacturing was employing an increasingly smaller proportion of our labor force and that the number of new manufacturing establishments created at new locations in any one year was fairly small. It was also clear that manufacturing was emigrating from historically dominant locations in the northeast and in central cities. Inquiry now seems to point to a markedly reciprocal relationship between population and manufacturing location. Population moves to jobs while manufacturing moves to markets. It also confirms the south and southwestern direction and suburban pattern of these locations. The meaning of "suburban" has tended to expand, however, to recognize that promixity measured in terms of the costs of time, not the costs of miles, is a better definition than the old one. Improvements in transportation have tended to expand the proportion of manufacturing firms that can locate relatively far from particular markets for inputs or outputs. This has tended to enhance the prospects for expansion of some smaller urban areas with good amenity endowments.

Urban areas have historically been the principal site of the non-manufacturing, service employments that employ growing shares of our productive labor
efforts. Attempts to understand the urban structure, the structure of the
dependent hinterland and their functioning and relationship to each other have
consumed significant attention in the last few years. A fuller understanding now
exists of the reasons for service employment concentration in urban areas, of the
interdependence of industries in urban areas, of the pattern of relationships
among cities of different sizes, and of the distinctive functions of communities
in that pattern of relationships. Notable progress has been made in delineating
the service and commutation areas, or "sheds," associated with urban centers.
This work has helped to explain the laggard development of much of Central
Appalachia, for example, which is the most heavily populated area in the nation
outside the commutation shed of major centers.

Several of these strands of understanding have woven together to alter the
evolving concept of the role of urban places in the development process. There
has been a revival of emphasis on the quality of local leadership. In disrepute as a
vestige of Babbitt-type boosterism for a long while, experience has tended to
suggest that the willingness of local "movers and shakers" to take a broad
geographic view, and consider long run implications, can have an important
influence on the prospects of their locality.

Not very long ago, the concept of a geographic growth center was taking hold
and analysts tended to view the city, the "center," as the locus and motive force
of growth. Investigation of spillover effects and commutation and service sheds
has led to the study of the entire field of urban-hinterland relationships, which
has tended to emphasize the strongly symbiotic relationships that exist.
Terminology increasingly has shifted to speak of growth areas rather than
centers, in recognition of these reciprocal dependencies. In a much broader sense
than merely as customers for its output and providers of economic inputs, the
prosperity and population characteristics of the hinterland strongly affect the
fortunes of the center.

Investigation and experience have led to a fuller understanding of the need
for a regional approach to the delivery of public services and of the role of these
services in influencing the fortunes of a region. There is now a better grasp of the
conditions that need to exist if a region is to be economically viable. And we
have developed a less rigid approach to the definition of a region. One result of
this has been increased dependence upon the context in which it is used to gain
an understanding of what the word "region" means. In some uses, a part of a
county is meant, in others, several states. Though there are still occasions for
defining non-overlapping regions on the basis of topography, other physical
conditions and historical data on economic and social activity, increasing
awareness has been evident that the configuration of a region is defined by the
problem at hand. Though administrative regions may be rigid, analytical regions
must be variable. The suitable region for the analysis of airport traffic is

different from the one employed in examining issues of law enforcement or solid waste disposal. The blending of results from investigations based on analytical boundaries into prescriptions that can be implemented for governmental and other institutions with their rigid borders requires the application of negotiative and persuasive skills of a high order. Those capable of doing so are some of the rarest resources for the process of economic development.

Other investigations conducted in these last few years focused on a better understanding of the impact of public investments and on the appropriate capacity to be built into them. Some of these have tried to trace the impacts of a single type of investment, such as a highway or an airport. Others have looked at groups composed of several types of investments. Generally, they have tried to assess the effect of changes in public facility availability on the costs of doing business. From this, estimates of overall economic effects are made. In some cases discernible effects have been found, in others not, though there has been a tendency to conclude that probably some such relationship does exist. Still others have approached the problem differently, inquiring when a shortage of public services, in other words, a bottleneck, would impede further economic development. Inquiries of this nature, and those attempting to develop a 15-year program plan and budget for the Appalachian Region, are adding to our ability to estimate when public and private actions will be required to achieve desired ends.

Undoubtedly as a result of the programs underway and the investigations they fostered, there has developed a growing recognition of the regional impacts of national policies. In passing the 1970 Rivers and Harbors Act, for example, Congress required that all water resources and related projects submitted to it contain evaluations of the regional development effects anticipated. Congress also wants information on the income redistribution and social well-being effects of these projects. The Water Resources Council has published standards and procedures designed to provide this information. There can be no doubt that this new emphasis on broader considerations was triggered, in part, by the evaluation techniques developed for the Appalachian Water Resources Survey.

By all these numerous small steps, progress has been made toward answers to the basic questions that are still far from fully answerable. Those questions, that relate to which public investments, in what sequence, with what timing, with what capacity, and at which locations, may never be precisely answerable but investigation and experience has added to what we know, including making suspect some things whose truth was formerly undoubted. All these investigations and experiences are based on a rather simple article of faith, however. They are based on the belief that economic development will add substance to the promise that individuals will have choices among alternative patterns of life. Wider choices, it is believed, provide the most felicitous opportunity for personal and social development. It is becoming increasingly evident that wisdom and creativity must be part of the development effort if that widening of opportunities is to be the ultimate effect. Economic development is a means, and not an end, and wisdom and creativity are required to keep that distinction clear and effectively influential in the programs the public undertakes.

Notes

Notes

Chapter 1
Introduction

1. S. 3381, the National Public Works Development Program, introduced March 21, 1972.

2. Address to the National Governors' Conference, February 23, 1972, page 1.

3. *Population and the American Future*, Part III, Chapter 12, Galleys 12-15 to 12-18 dated March 24, 1972.

Chapter 2
The Appalachian Experience: A Factual Background

1. Plus five independent cities in Virginia that are each physically contained within counties included in the Region.

2. *Appalachia*, A Report by the President's Appalachian Regional Commission, Washington, D.C., G.P.O., 1964, Table C-12.

3. *Appalachia*, Vol. 4, No. 6, March-April 1971, p. 30.

4. Section 2, Appalachian Regional Development Act of 1965 (ARDA).

5. Section 224, ARDA.

6. The following discussion draws in part upon material prepared for the Commission's own evaluation mentioned in the Preface. It is designed to provide a descriptive background that will be reviewed later to highlight implications.

7. An exception is the allocation formula for Sec. 202 which was adopted in September 1971.

Chapter 3
Past Policies and the Appalachian Condition

1. See *Appalachia*, Vol. 4, No. 6, March-April 1971, p. 12.

2. In recognition of this, the Emergency Employment Act of 1971 creates a system of public *service* employment for the unemployed and underemployed during periods of excessive unemployed.

3. James Sundquist, *Making Federalism Work*, The Brookings Institution, 1969.

4. The members of PARC, in addition to Mr. Roosevelt and Mr. Whisman were representatives of the Governors of Alabama, Georgia, Kentucky, Maryland, North Carolina, Pennsylvania, Tennessee, Virginia, and West Virginia

(though included in the Region, Ohio did not participate) plus the representatives of the Secretaries of Health, Education and Welfare, Treasury, Defense, Labor, Interior, Agriculture, and Commerce, the Chairmen of the Atomic Energy Commission and the Tennessee Valley Authority, and the Administrators of the Small Business Administration, National Aeronautics and Space Administration, and Area Redevelopment Administration.

5. *Appalachia*, A Report By the President's Appalachian Regional Commission, GPO, Washington, D.C., 1964 (PARC Report).

6. The following has been drawn from material prepared for the Commission's evaluation report.

7. Page 19.

Chapter 4
Conceptual Bases of an Appalachian Program

1. It has since been estimated that 8% of the structural unemployment in 1964 was regional in nature. Barbara Bergmann and David E. Kaun, *Structural Unemployment in the United States*, U.S. Department of Commerce, Economic Development Administration, 1966.

2. Research in Appalachia has suggested that for that region, import substitution opportunities may be small until the entire level of economic activity is increased. See *The Spartial Concentration of Industry in Appalachia*, Research Report No. 9, Appendix B, Appalachian Regional Commission, especially p. 89.

3. Hildebrand and Mace, "Employment Multipliers . . .," *Review of Economics and Statistics*, Vol. 32 (1950).

4. Page 19.

5. French indicative planning is an example of an attempt to implement this approach.

Chapter 5
Strategies for Appalachian Development

1. An earlier version of this material was prepared for the ARC evaluation.

2. A commentary on the process of refining a program's strategy while it is in operation can be found in Ralph R. Widner, "Political Implementation of Regional Theory in Appalachia," *Growth and Change*, Vol. 2, No. 1, January 1971.

3. See John Friedmann, "Poor Regions and Poor Nations: Perspectives on the Problem of Appalachia," *Southern Economic Journal*, Vol. 32, No. 4, April 1966.

4. A partial measure of the degree to which this anticipation has been realized can be found in the fact that out of about 2400 projects submitted, the states have been asked to withdraw only about 100.

5. It should be noted, however, that innovations were recommended for some established programs, such as the criteria used to allocate funds for highways and the use of general revenues, rather than trust fund monies, to finance their construction. Some other recommendations, such as Federal subsidies for health care programs to cover their operating deficits did not suggest Federal entry into entirely new fields but were so novel that the term "innovation" could well be applied to them.

6. The legislative history of the Act is discussed extensively in Rothblatt, *Regional Planning: The Appalachian Experience*, D.C. Heath, Lexington, Mass.

7. Advisory Commission on Intergovernmental Relations, *Urban and Rural American: Politics for Future Growth*, 1968.

8. Resolution of Nov. 30, 1966.

9. *The Appalachian Regional Commission Code* established on Nov. 30, 1966.

10. The complex criteria for development highway projects cannot be summarized briefly and are discussed in Chapter 7.

Chapter 6
Planning for Appalachian Development

1. Highway funds are omitted from this comparison because the combination of Federal and State influences has given the Commission little choice but to press for the completion of the highway system, substantially as originally outlined by PARC, even if it wished otherwise.

2. *Evaluation of Timber Development Organizations*, Research Report No. 1.

3. *Guidelines for an Appalachian Airport System*, Research Report No. 3.

4. In the area covered by the ARC airport plan, of the 41 projects funded by FAA is fiscal 1971, 28 conformed to the plan.

5. See *Report on Regional Action Planning Program*, A.D. Little, Inc., June 5, 1970.

6. Pp. 39-41.

7. *Preliminary Analysis for Development of Central Appalachia*, Research Report Nos. 8 and 9.

8. *Recreation as an Industry*, Research Report No. 2.

9. *Recreation Potential in the Appalachian Highlands: A Market Analysis*, Research Report No. 14.

10. The next 7 paragraphs are substantially as prepared for inclusion in the Commission's evaluation report. For a more detailed discussion of the evolution

and content of each State Plan, see Volume 3 of that report as well as the Commission's *State and Regional Development Plans in Appalachia, 1968.*

11. For a description of one districts' activities, see "Pennsylvania's Turnpike Development District Sets Priorities for Growth," *Appalachia*, January 1971, Vol. 4, No. 4, pp. 1-10.

Chapter 7
Organization for Appalachian Development

1. Donald M. Rothblatt, *Regional Planning: The Appalachian Experience.* This book contains the fullest description of the allocation formulas generally available.

2. For a critical review of the allocation of funds to and within the development highway program, see John M. Munroe, "Planning the Appalachian Highway System: Some Critical Questions." *Land Economics*, Vol. 45, No. 2, May 1969 and the letter of reply by Ralph R. Widner, reprinted in Hansen, *A Review of the Appalachian Regional Commission*, Univ. of Texas, Nov. 1969, Appendix I. See also the Commission's *Highway Transportation and Appalachian Development*, Research Report No. 13 and Government Accounting Office, *Highway Program Shows Limited Progress Toward Increasing Accessibility To and Through Appalachia*.

3. Data collected in the field and reports prepared by ARC staff following their field work were used extensively in this section.

4. At the time of this writing, there were 54 district organizations in operation, leaving 16 districts without an organized unit. Eleven of the latter were in West Virginia which was in the process of re-vamping its former organizational structure and had terminated groups that had formerly operated. In addition to all the counties in West Virginia, eleven Appalachian counties were not in organized districts—6 in Kentucky, 1 each in Mississippi and Tennessee, and 3 in New York.

5. The average staff size is 7 which may be only slightly more than the minimum size for efficiency and effectiveness.

6. A similar discussion of some of this material appears in Volume 4 of the Commission's evaluation report.

Chapter 8
Program Expenditures for Appalachian Development

1. Clearly, this applied to that large majority of cases in which the corridor location of a development highway followed that of an existing road.

2. An exception was made for the relatively rare, but conceivable, cases in

mountainous terrain when the cost of four lane construction can be less than that for two lane construction.

3. Less $35 million then set aside for access roads.

4. As previously mentioned, when New York entered the Region, development highway mileage was obtained for it. The entrance of Mississippi did not lead to an expansion of the Congressional authorized highway mileage nor did the other States make part of their previously allocated mileage available to the new member.

5. The logic of the ARC investment strategy helps assure this. Investments are located to serve where growth may occur. Growth is related to access. Consequently, facilities are centered around places receiving access improvements. Roughly 70% of ARC projects are within 5 miles of a high quality highway.

6. Appalachian Regional Commission, *1970 Annual Report*, p. 80.

7. Such an approach was recommended by the General Accounting Office in its *Limited Progress*, op. cit.

8. They "will serve specific recreational, residential, educational, commercial, industrial or like facilities or will facilitate a school consolidation program."

9. *Capitalizing on New Development*, Research Report No. 11.

10. These are reported in its Research Report No. 13, op. cit.

11. J.M. Munro, op. cit., Niles Hansen, "Neglected Factors in American Regional Development Policy: The Case of Appalachia," *Land Economics*, February 1966.

12. Taken from material prepared for the Commission's internal evaluation.

13. This led to the termination of allocations of Section 205 funds. It was agreed that virtually all available funds would be used in Pennsylvania and that the state would not be penalized for this by a reduction in funds under other sections of the Act.

14. These limitations were to be expected since Congress had only recently agreed to the passage of the Elementary and Secondary School Act.

15. The Committee may have viewed ARC as primarily interested in economic development and labored under the misconception that a broader recommendation would not have been appreciated.

16. P. 60.

17. *Status of Secondary Vocational Education in Appalachia*, Research Report No. 10.

18. *Appalachia, Education for Tomorrow*—Summary and Recommendations of the Education Advisory Committee to the Appalachian Regional Commission.

19. *Teachers in Appalachia*, Research Report No. 12.

20. The ARC's major effort involving early childhood programs has been reserved for discussion in the section on health which follows on p. 140.

21. 1970 Annual Report, p. 70.

22. The Commission lists activities under seven headings: recreation, health,

environment, housing, education, economic development, human resource development, transportation, and political-legal. Ibid., p. 72.

23. Ibid.

24. Health care investments, other than those under Section 202, are reserved for the next section of this chapter.

25. As of September 1971, the Commission decided to allocate Section 202 funds under a formula that is similar to those used for other sections of the Act and that also recognizes the funding requirements of programs already initiated.

26. Obviously, the same individual may be counted more than once in these statistics.

27. In part, this section contains material prepared for the Commission's internal evaluation.

Chapter 9
Appraisal and Prospects

1. The Commission's report of its inquiry will be presented in Volume 3 of this evaluation report.

2. Investments excluded are mostly those under Section 201-a (development highway), Section 202 (health), Section 302 (research and local development district funding) and certain grants serving large areas (such as those for educational TV), the precise location of which is irrelevant.

3. It is estimated that ARC has exercised influence over about 3% of the federal funds flowing to the region.

4. If Tennessee were omitted from Central Appalachia in this table, that area would show little growth in employment.

5. The material in this section was derived from field research reported in Volume 3 of the ARC evaluation.

6. Ibid.

7. See U.S. Dept. of Commerce, Economic Development Administration, *A Study of the Effects of Public Investment*, May 1969.

8. National Goals Research Staff, *Toward Balanced Growth: Quantity with Quality*, G.P.O., July 4, 1970.

9. See, for example, Regional Planning Issues, Hearings before the subcommittee on Urban Affairs, Joint Economic Committee, 92nd Cong., 1st Session and Advisory Commission on Intergovernmental Relations, *Urban and Rural America: Policies for Future Growth*, April 1968.

10. This point was made with scholarly force in James Sundquist's *Making Federalism Work*, The Brookings Institution, 1969 and with political force in the 1971 State of the Union Address in which President Nixon recommended the establishment of revenue sharing. It has found legislative expression in Title VII of the Housing and Urban Development Act of 1970 that calls for the

establishment of a national urban growth policy and the submission of annual reports by the President.

11. The history of earlier legislative support is well covered in Rothblatt, op. cit. More recently, the Senate voted to extend the ARDA by votes of 77-3 and 88-2 in 1971, the President said "I support the Appalachian program 100%" when he vetoed the first bill passed in 1971 to extend it (as recounted in Chapter I), and Congress has incorporated the development highway idea into law by creating "Economic Growth Center Development Highways" in the Federal-Aid Highway Act of 1970. The concept of a state plan was included in the Economic Disaster Relief Act of 1971 proposed in that year, for example. The bill called for each state to produce a State Full Employment and Economic Recovery Plan.

Index

About the Author

Monroe Newman joined the Appalachian development program in 1964 and after two years on the staff has remained connected with it as its Special Consultant on Advanced Planning. He is Professor of Economics at The Pennsylvania State University. He was appointed to the faculty there in 1955 and has served as Head of the Department of Economics and as Chairman of the Graduate Program in Regional Planning.

He received his B.A. from Antioch College and his M.A. and Ph.D. from the University of Illinois.